CW00349951

## THEY'RE USING

# Osram
**LAMPS**

## ON BOARD

Your favourite lamps are
helping to bring Victory

*It m̶a̶k̶e̶s̶ ̶y̶o̶u̶*
*feel you need*
*a bath"*

What luxury after a ' sticky interlude '—
the refreshment of Wright's fragrant
lather; the gentle cleansing! You're
fresh and fit again; protected invisibly
from infection wherever you go.

*For protection against infection*

*- always use*

# WRIGHT'S
*Coal Tar Soap*

7½d. per tablet. Purchase Tax Included.

WJ.

# LILLIPUT
# Goes to War

*edited by*
# KAYE WEBB

Hutchinson
London Melbourne Sydney Auckland Johannesburg

Hutchinson & Co. (Publishers) Ltd

An imprint of Century Hutchinson Ltd

17–21 Conway Street, London W1P 6JD

Hutchinson Publishing Group (Australia) Pty Ltd
16–22 Church Street, Hawthorn, Melbourne, Victoria 3122

Hutchinson Group (NZ) Ltd
32–34 View Road, PO Box 40–086, Glenfield, Auckland 10

Hutchinson Group (SA) Pty Ltd
PO Box 337, Bergvlei 2012, South Africa

First published in this selection 1985
This selection © Kaye Webb 1985

Filmset in Monophoto Bembo and printed by Jolly & Barber Ltd, Rugby

Bound in Great Britain by Anchor Brendon Ltd, Tiptree, Essex

British Library Cataloguing in Publication Data
Lilliput goes to war.
 1. Great Britain——Social conditions——20th
century——Sources
 I. Webb, Kaye
 941.084    HN385

ISBN 0 90 161760 X

# Preface

LILLIPUT first appeared in August 1937. It was the result of a meeting between Alison Blair and Stefan Lorant, the brilliant, volatile Hungarian who was among the earliest of the many writers, artists and photographers who came to Britain from Europe as the menace of Hitler's fascism increased. Lorant wanted to produce a new general-interest magazine small enough to fit into a pocket; Alison found the money and they started it together.

The first issue cost 6d., had over 100 pages and a combination of lively articles, stories and cartoons, as well as the photographic jokes (the juxtapositions or doubles) which became one of the little magazine's best-known features.

Because of Stefan Lorant's background, the magazine was one of the first, if not the very first, to lace its contents with warnings concerning the immediate threat of war. Very early in 1938, doubles about Hitler and his cronies Goebbels and Göring were appearing, as well as serious and knowledgeable articles about Britain's state of readiness for war, side by side with jokes and stories on the same theme.

A few months later when, ironically, the very success of *Lilliput* was raising financial problems, the two founder editors were joined by Sydney Jacobson, who invested his own savings in it. The situation continued to be financially precarious, but the three editors resolutely kept up the quality of the magazine, considering, as Sydney Jacobson wrote in the hundredth issue, 'that the public is more intelligent, has a keener sense of humour and likes better pictures and drawings than most journalists, publishers and politicians believe'. It was in 1939, when they were simply unable to pay for the next huge print order, that Sir Edward Hulton, who wanted a grant to start *Picture Post*, bought both *Lilliput* and its editors, and their cheerful independence ended. But the three of them continued to work in happy unison until the increasing demands of the war made that impossible, and from 1941 until 1946 *Lilliput* was edited by Tom Hopkinson (who was also editing *Picture Post*), with myself as assistant editor.

As the war got under way, *Lilliput* quickly became a favourite with the

Forces, partly because of its size and relatively undemanding text, but equally because of its jokes and occasional nudes, and many unsolicited stories and articles reached our office. Equally, because of paper rationing and the consequent shortage of other outlets, we found ourselves able to publish many distinguished writers of that time, including G. B. Shaw, H. G. Wells, Arthur Koestler, V. S. Pritchett and Max Beerbohm. For reasons of space, some of these have had to be left out of this selection, but I have included one or two historic 'firsts' – Gerard Hoffnung as an aspiring schoolboy, C. S. Forester's rare short story, Henry Moore's Underground drawings, Bill Brandt's dazzling records of the London Blitz and Ronald Searle's first St Trinian's cartoon.

This collection does not attempt to present itself as the best of a magazine which was published successfully for twenty-five years, for its character and contents changed significantly after the world was at peace again. But it has seemed worthwhile making a selection of those items which reflected, however light-heartedly, the involvement of all our citizens in wartime, from the frustrations of appeasement in 1938 until the surrender of Japan eight years later. So I have concentrated on the war as it affected the domestic life of our country and as it conveyed something of the spirit of those days. For those younger readers who may be interested in it as a piece of history, I append a short list of some of the more significant dates.

*Kaye Webb, 1985*

## SOME RELEVANT DATES

1937 Nov. Air Raid Precautions bill
1938 Feb. Hitler becomes War Minister Anthony Eden resigns
Aug. Germany mobilises
Nov. Anti-semitic pogrom in Germany and Italy
Dec. British National Register for War Service
1939 Mar. Britain and France pledge support to Poland
Apr. Conscription for men aged twenty to twenty-one
Aug. Evacuation of women and children from London

(3rd) Sept. Britain declares war on Germany
National Service bill: conscription of men between nineteen and forty-one
Identity cards issued
1940 Jan. Food rationing
May Chamberlain resigns; Churchill forms National Government
Home Guard formed
British forces evacuated from Dunkirk
June France capitulates

4

| | | |
|---|---|---|
| | July | Ninety German bombers shot down over Britain |
| | Aug. | All-night raids on London |
| | Nov. | Blitz continues, 4,558 people killed in month in Britain |
| 1941 | Mar. | London air raids resumed |
| | Apr. | Blitz on Coventry |
| | June | Clothes rationing begins |
| | Aug. | National Fire Service established |
| | Nov. | British begin attack in Western Desert |
| | Dec. | Japanese bomb Pearl Harbor – America enters the war Call-up age lowered to eighteen |
| 1942 | Jan. | Japanese invade Burma |
| | Feb. | Singapore surrenders |
| | Apr. | Eighth Army retreats to El Alamein |
| | Oct. | Battle of El Alamein |
| | Nov. | Rommel in full retreat |
| 1943 | Jan | Air bombing of London renewed Eighth Army enters Tripoli |
| | Feb. | General Eisenhower takes command in North Africa RAF bombs Berlin |
| | Mar. | Montgomery breaks Mareth Line |
| | Apr. | Rommel retreats. British forces link up. Massacre in Warsaw Ghetto |
| | July | Allies land in Sicily |
| | Sept. | Italy surrenders |
| | Nov. | Churchill, Stalin and Roosevelt hold Teheran conference |
| 1944 | Jan. | RAF drops 2,300 tons of bombs on Berlin Allied landings at Anzio |
| | Feb. | Air raids on London heaviest since 1941 |
| | Mar. | Daylight bombing of Berlin by USA |
| | May | Allies break through Hitler Line in Italy |

| | | |
|---|---|---|
| | June | Fifth Army enters Rome D-Day landings in Normandy Flying-bombs dropped on London |
| | July | Attempt to assassinate Hitler |
| | Aug. | Warsaw rising British land in French Riviera General de Gaulle enters Paris |
| | Sept. | First V-2 rocket lands in Britain Black-out restrictions relaxed |
| | Nov. | Roosevelt wins USA Presidential Election |
| | Dec. | Battle of the Bulge North Burma cleared of Japanese |
| 1945 | Feb. | Yalta Conference: Churchill, Stalin, Roosevelt British troops reach Rhine USA air raids on Tokyo |
| | Mar. | Last of 1,050 V-2 rockets |
| | Apr. | Roosevelt dies. Truman becomes President of USA Allies enter Arnhem Russians reach Berlin Mussolini killed by partisans Hitler dies in Berlin |
| | May | German army surrenders in Italy Berlin surrenders to the Russians V-E Day Churchill forms Conservative 'caretaker' ministry |
| | June | Allied Control Commission assumes control throughout Germany |
| | July | Labour landslide in General Election |
| | Aug. | USA drops atomic bomb on Hiroshima and Nagasaki Japan surrenders – end of Second World War |

For Alison Blair who caused *Lilliput* to happen

*"Yes, LILLIPUT speaking"*

ASZMANN

BUDAPEST

*The not-impossible she*
*(Lilliput's first nude)*

## By Ernest Hemingway

## A Story from Spain

AN old man with steel-rimmed spectacles and very dusty clothes sat by the side of the road. There was a pontoon bridge across the river and carts, trucks, and men, women and children were crossing it. The mule-drawn carts staggered up the steep bank from the bridge with soldiers helping push against the spokes of the wheels. The trucks ground up and away, heading out of it all, and the peasants plodded along in the ankle-deep dust.

But the old man sat there without moving. He was too tired to go any farther.

It was my business to cross the bridge, explore the bridgehead beyond and find out to what point the enemy had advanced. I did this and returned over the bridge. The old man was still there.

"Where do you come from?" I asked him.   "From San Carlos," he said, and smiled.

That was his native town and so it gave him pleasure to mention it, and he smiled.

"I was taking care of animals," he explained.

"Oh," I said, not quite understanding.

"Yes," he said, "I stayed, you see, taking care of animals. I was the last one to leave the town of San Carlos."

He did not look like a shepherd nor a herdsman, and I looked at his black, dusty clothes and his grey, dusty face and his steel-rimmed spectacles and said, "What animals were they?"

"Various animals," he said. "I had to leave them."

I was watching the bridge and the African-looking country of the Ebro Delta and wondering how long now it would be before we would see the enemy, and listening all the while for the first noises that would signal that ever mysterious event called contact, and the old man still sat there.

"What animals were they?" I asked again.

"There were three animals altogether," he explained. "There were two goats and a cat and then there were four pairs of pigeons."

"And you had to leave them?"

"Yes. Because of the artillery. The captain told me to go because of the artillery."

"And you have no family?" I asked, watching the far end of the bridge where a few last carts were hurrying down the bank.

"No," he said, "only the animals I stated. The cat, of course, will be all right. A cat can look out for itself, but I cannot think what will become of the others."

"What politics have you?" I asked.

"I am without politics," he said. "I am 76 years old. I have come 12 kilometres now and I think now I can go no farther."

"This is not a good place to stop," I said. "If you can make it, there are trucks up the road where it forks for Tortosa."

"I will wait a while," he said, "and then I will go. Where do the trucks go?"

"Towards Barcelona."

"I know of no one in that direction," he said, "but thank you very much."

He looked at me very blankly and tiredly, then said, having to share his worry with someone, "The cat will be all right, I am sure. There is no need to be unquiet about the cat. But the others. Now what do you think about the others?"

"Why, they'll probably come through it all right."

"You think so?"

"Why not?" I said, watching the far bank where now there were no carts.

"But what will they do under the artillery when I was told to leave because of the artillery?"

"Did you leave the dove cage unlocked?" I asked.

"Yes."

"Then they'll fly."

"Yes, certainly they'll fly. But the others. It's better not to think about the others," he said.

"If you are rested I would go," I urged. "Get up and try now."

"Thank you," he said, and got to his feet, swayed from side to side, and then sat down backwards in the dust.

"I was taking care of animals," he said dully, but no longer to me. "I was only taking care of animals."

There was nothing to do about him. The Fascists were advancing toward the Ebro. It was a grey, overcast day with a low ceiling, so their planes were not up.

That, and the fact that cats know how to look after themselves, was all the good luck that old man would ever have.

MAN                                                                                            london

*Choose your news*

# POLITICS

By Lucien Zacharoff

# What Will the Next War Be Like?

SOMEONE said that "War is the continuation of diplomacy by other means." We have had plenty of interesting diplomacy in the last few years. Hadn't we better be looking forward to what the war, when it comes, will be like?

Pacifists wave their hands in the air and make quaint noises, but the size of standing armies, in Western Europe alone, has increased twenty per cent. between 1925 and 1934. Simultaneously there has been a staggering growth in the membership of semi-military organisations, particularly where Fascist and militarist dictatorships hold sway. In Germany last year there were twelve times more men in such disguised armed forces than in the Reichswehr.

Millions of units of cannon fodder are feverishly drilling. Exceeding by far the number of participants in the world war, they are provided with mightily advanced war technique and equipment. Germany alone will have in the field 300 divisions, 10,000 tanks, 7,500 airplanes.

Artillery will come into its own in the next war. In the last one there were four guns to every 1,000 soldiers; now there are eight. The only recognisable thing about modern artillery is its name; new models have unprecedented power, are mechanically propelled, and can penetrate hitherto impassable regions. The shelling of Paris from a distance of about 40 miles was the first application of super-range artillery, but the range of a shell has been stepped up as much as 160 per cent. since 1914.

Aviation is occupying a place of honour in armament. The number of first-line planes in England, Germany, France, Japan, Italy and United States has grown tenfold since 1925. Of all means of modern warfare, aviation has the greatest range. In the world war cities like Berlin and Rome were never subjected to aerial bombardment. To-day, not a single country in Europe has territory immune from air-raids. For the heaviest modern planes the cruising range is 600 miles and more; the distance between Berlin

> **THE BALANCE SHEET OF THE WORLD WAR:**
>
> | | |
> |---|---:|
> | Killed .. .. .. .. .. | 9,998,771 |
> | Heavily wounded .. .. .. | 6,295,512 |
> | Lightly wounded .. .. .. | 14,002,039 |
> | Missing, including prisoners of war and those mutilated beyond recognition.. | 5,983,600 |
> | Died in 1918 in the 'flu epidemic brought on by the war .. .. .. about | 10,000,000 |
>
> This estimate does not mention millions of war widows and orphans, nor millions of minds permanently impaired, the social, economic and cultural havoc which set us back by generations.

and London is less than 600 miles, a mere hop nowadays.

Simultaneously with the range there has grown the "useful" load capacity of the bombing plane. The combined discharge of explosives from 300 heavy bombers is greater than the united salvo of all the guns in Britain's Navy. Special attention is given to developing air armadas capable of carrying to the *rear* of the enemy lines thousands of tons of bombs. To make the bombers less vulnerable to anti-aircraft guns, their flying altitude has been raised close to the stratosphere.

Modern military aviation boasts of planes that lift twelve tons of bomb cargo. Think what a group of ten such carriers of death can do! They would find plentiful targets among the women and children and the industrial and cultural centres of the world.

A new manner of fighting has been created by aviation in another sense: a tribe of fighters consisting of parachuting expeditionary forces lands in the rear of the enemy troops. Floating down to earth where least expected, the parachutists may seize and destroy important railroad centres, sources of electric and industrial energy. After descending on an enemy aerodrome, they can act as hosts to their own aircraft, which will bring light tanks, light armoured automobiles, artillery, and trucks to turn a parachuting force into a motor detachment.

Speed of land-troop movements is not neglected either. Modern tanks are far ahead of the veterans of 1914 in engines, armour plate, and speed. Tanks nowadays weigh as much as sixty to seventy-five tons. They carry heavy artillery and dozens of machine-guns each. Many of them overcome obstacles such as bodies of water and ditches fifteen to twenty feet wide.

In future battles while the infantry is being attacked at the front, aviation and tanks will harass the reserves in the rear, impregnable and speedy tanks will smash through to the artillery positions to silence the enemy guns, parachuting forces will be landed behind the front lines to cut communications, the entire resources of the enemy will be broken up and annihilated separately. The civilian population cannot escape because it is clustered about industrial centres and railroad junctions which will be the first to be destroyed.

Military chemistry has evolved novel poison horrors to be utilised on a mass scale. Modern chemistry makes possible liquid poisons which evaporate slowly and act on the victim's skin, breathing, and sight. Cities and regions are turned into gaseous swamps in which life is possible only in masks and special impenetrable clothing.

Other chemical contributions include substances creating heat capable of melting steel, substances which are unyielding to ordinary fire-fighting.

Bacteriological warfare recommends itself for its quickness of action and inexpensiveness. Contagion-carrying materials manufacture themselves, so to speak. To be sure, the nation which uses this method takes a great risk, since self-defence against the worst forms of contagion has not been perfected.

How will bacteria be distributed? The simplest of a number of plans is to have aeroplanes drop glass tubes filled with contagious germs, or parachute-equipped animals infected with some plague or other. Bacteriological warfare must be used cautiously in crowded Europe, but such methods could easily be applied against isolated nations.

Let the Man in the Street ponder on the enormous costs of the last conflict, and of the current dress rehearsals, costs which cannot even be guessed for the next war. But one thing is certain : the bloody rampage to come will concern him much more directly and exquisitely.

JOHN HEARTFIELD

LONDON

*Masterpieces of political art*
*"Kaiser Adolf"*
*This striking satire of Leader-worship is typical of the work of John Heartfield, the*
*German photo-montage expert. Combining photographs of the ex-Kaiser and Hitler,*
*he has given Hitler the upturned moustaches, plumed helmet and gorgeous uniform of Wilhelm II.*

JOHN HEARTFIELD

LONDO

*Masterpieces of political art*
*Butter for everyone*
*This bitterly satirical comment on Goering's famous remark, "Guns are better than butter" shows a German family eating metal for their meal.*

### By Naomi Mitchison

# I Have Five Children

I HAVE five children, and to-day is like 1914. I am sure that war is not yet inevitable. But certain possibilities must be faced.

In 1914, we could blame our elders and betters who had led us up the Liberal garden path, crazy-paved with good intentions. But now we are, partly at least, to blame ourselves.

After all, it was we who were so happy when the fighting was over, so occupied with nursing back to ordinary life war-hurt brothers and husbands, that we just never noticed what was going on at Versailles, and never noticed when we and our allies suppressed the workers' movements to overthrow the old gangs in Germany, Austria, Hungary and elsewhere, which might really have made that "world safe for democracy" about which we had all been talking and hoping. Instead of noticing, and being particularly wary of what the politicians were doing behind our backs, we settled down to being all domestic again; we had babies.

And now those peace babies are growing up and seeing the mess that has been made for them.

We didn't care for politics. We left it to the experts. And now a fine vintage of sour grapes is setting the children's teeth on edge. Most of us had friends in Vienna . . . I had. I only know there is no news of them.

My eldest boy is eighteen. He is aware of what is happening in the outside world, beyond the lovely walls of the University, and also why those happenings have come, in a way that my generation did not begin to be. He is a scientist; the world needs them, and will do so increasingly as its needs get clearer. I have tried not to force any point of view upon him, though equally I have never hidden what seems to me to be nearest the truth.

I believe that he would fight in a war against Fascism and the Totalitarian idea, but only if that war had a chance of achieving its end—and he is well aware that any war would be said to be a war "for democracy," "in defence of the League," and all that. He would have to have some very thorough guarantee, something more than speeches in Parliament, before he would fight.

However "righteous" a war was, I would keep him out of it, and all the other eighteen-year-olds, if I possibly could. But I must not, and cannot, decide for him. I have seen one generation of honourable and gentle young men caught up by a war which seemed righteous to them, and which made a worse world at the end than at the beginning. I know how inevitably the individual is made worse, and not better, by war. If he survives.

Yet there are, I know, certain moments in human history when a situation so intolerable arises that the only way out is by war. But I hope with all my heart that neither my boy nor the others will be duped into fighting for other people's moneybags.

The rest of the children are not yet at an age to be faced with the dilemma of using a bad means for a doubtful end, or of conscientious objection—which will be much harder for the objectors now than it was during the last war. My two youngest are at home; I try not to let them see how frightened I sometimes am for them—but probably they do see, but, like good modern children, they are kind to their poor parents, and pretend

not to notice. They are not afraid themselves. They have no experience to be afraid with.

Oddly enough, I'm not really frightened of being killed myself. I would even, if necessary, kill, though not under the directions of any of my present rulers. I have had a good and full life; I have done or experienced most of the sort of things which are worth while. I have been happier than most people; I have always accepted any adventures which came my way; I haven't been a cautious one.

I *am* frightened of being hurt, but that's only sense; it would be annoying to be killed in the middle of something one wants to do, but why should one fear death for oneself?

But I feel that my children are more myself than I am; if one of them were to be killed I would experience that as the bitterness of death, that as the intolerably frightening thing. In spite of what I know through my intelligence, yet, like other mothers, I believe in my heart that my children are immortal. It seems impossible that this sweet flesh should ever decay. I cannot separate my love and my fear.

I have five children. And I keep on thinking, with sickening and violent sympathy and realisation,

KEYSTONE

LONDON

*This Chinese mother, too, had five children*

of mothers in Spain and China who *had* five children. The aeroplanes come . . . what, all my pretty chickens? . . . at one fell swoop?

I love those children, too, and I have seen *their* sweet flesh mangled and pierced with small holes; small, iron-drilled holes, big enough for their purpose. Honour to the Spanish Government which has not bombed children. Dishonour for ever to Franco and his allies: dishonour to Japan. They have deliberately committed the most hopeless sin of which even humanity is capable—even this species of ours which kills its fellows, not for hunger or love, but for profit and glory. The Spanish rebels have erased the word pity from their vocabulary, and are proud of it; no doubt they have also erased the word love.

I have five children, and they are in danger from the murderous madness of an idea that has got loose in Europe: the idea that the individual does not matter, but only the state : the old Moloch idea which has menaced mothers before.

My instinct is to run, to hide them. But that will not save the other children of other mothers. I have to attack that idea whenever and wherever I see it as attackable and destructible. I have to set against it the counter-idea of the love of all children, all of them potentially good men and women, love translated into economic practice, but always based on the tenderness that individuals should have for one another. Individual people, so easily hurt, with only their skins between them and the world, unarmoured, looking out through eyes that a grain of sand can fill with pain. It is fantastic that such creatures should have put so much of their intelligence into inventing new ways of hurting one another.

Unless we can change the world, and that soon, it will be no place for children. We cannot change it through fear, but we can and will change it through love.

I want a new world for my five children.

"*The aeroplanes come* . . ."
*A drawing by a Spanish child*

**DANGER**

# Lilliput In Germany

The Editor,
''Lilliput''

Dear Sir,

     As I am of the confirmed opinion that ''Lilliput'' is the best entertainment for any long journey; it may interest you to know that having fallen asleep just before crossing the border into Germany and therefore failing to carry out my intention of disposing of this Magazine (as even you will agree, the June issue was a little strong for the Nazi palate!) I had an extremely uncomfortable 10 minutes trying to convince the Customs Officers that I had no intention whatsoever of trying to smuggle this book into Germany.

     It was not until the carriage had been thoroughly searched and swept and the Magazine confiscated, that they withdrew, leaving two somewhat wiser but slightly disgruntled Englishwomen!

     If there is any moral to be drawn from this incident may I hasten to forestall you in saying that he (or she) who possesses a ''Lilliput'' should never <u>wish</u> to sleep!

     Long may you cause confusion.

31 Herbert Rd.,
    S.E.18.

*Eunice Burrew*

# What They Cost

| | |
|---|---|
| Singapore Naval Base.. | £11,211,750 |
| 35,000 ton Battleship.. | £7,142,000 |
| Boeing B 15 Warplane | £400,000 |
| 1,090 ton Submarine .. | £349,750 |
| 16 in. Naval Gun .. | £45,000 |
| 35 ton Land Tank .. | £25,000 |
| Multi-engined Bomber | £20,000 |
| Single-engine Warplane | £6,250 |
| Naval Torpedo .. | £2,000 |
| 4.7 in. Gun .. .. | £1,520 |
| Vickers Machine Gun | £200 |
| One round 16 in. Shell | £200 |
| Lewis Gun .. .. | £60 |
| Irvin Silk Parachute .. | £60 |
| "Standard" Air Raid Shelter .. .. | £8 15s. |
| Service Rifle .. .. | £8 |
| One round 4.7 in..Shell | £6 |
| Civilian Gas Mask .. | 2s. 6d. |

## By A. J. Cummings

# The Cost of a Mistake

WHOSE mistake was it? Not that of any individual statesman or any particular Government.

The responsibility belongs to successive British and French Governments. Allied diplomacy in the years after the signing of the Peace Treaty failed almost entirely to understand the basic fact that the best hope of establishing a stable peace in Europe lay in the maintenance of a democratic and reasonably prosperous Germany.

The disregard, by France in particular, of clauses in the Versailles Treaty pledging the victorious nations to a policy of disarmament at the same time that the German military machine was compulsorily reduced to the smallest compass; the prolonged exaction of uneconomic reparations; the insistence on a war guilt consciousness as a reason for denying the approach to German equality of status in Europe—these and other melancholy consequences of victory in war not only brought bankruptcy and human suffering to Germany, but filled her people with humiliation and resentment.

The most hopeful post-war period of appeasement was that in which Sir Austen Chamberlain, M. Briand and Herr Stresemann co-operated in the formulation of the Locarno Treaties. Their personal co-operation appeared to mark the beginnings of goodwill and political understanding. But action lagged behind goodwill, partly because French suspicions were not stilled and partly because of the stubborn conviction that Germany could be made to pay for the war without economic disaster.

It was these mistakes and this illusion which made possible, if not inevitable, Hitler's rise to power. Up to 1930 Hitler was something of a joke. Thereafter he was an "immense phenomenon."

Even as late as June, 1931, when Dr. Brüning, Stresemann's successor as the German Chancellor, came to England to discuss with Mr. Ramsay MacDonald, Labour Prime Minister, the immediate problem of Germany's critical financial position, his warnings were not taken seriously by either British or French statesmen.

He said then, and he was passionately in earnest, that unless Germany received adequate assistance Hitler would come into power and Europe would be compelled to rearm. His prediction was received by those who heard it with amused scepticism. Brüning returned to Berlin, without credits or credit, a doomed man, knowing that he could not save German democracy.

He tried to govern by decree. His emergency measures taxed the German people, rich and poor, to the uttermost limit. In an almost despairing manifesto, President von Hindenburg declared to the world that "the limit of privations which we can impose on our nation has been reached."

All to no purpose. There was no more money for the Allies and no more hope for the German people. In the following year at Lausanne reparations came virtually to an end. In the words of Mr. John Wheeler-Bennett, who

wrote the history of the Lausanne Agreement, it had taken the statesmen a fatal thirteen years and thirty-five conferences to discover the truth which Professor Keynes preached in 1919; and the discovery was only brought about by a process of *reductio ad absurdum*.

The history of reparations is the "story of a prolonged series of economic experiments with Germany as a subject, a species of economic vivisection." The experiments were abandoned too late to save Brüning and democratic Germany. Her fate, like his, was already sealed.

The "immense phenomenon" of Hitler is transforming the face of Europe.

Our mistakes — above all, perhaps, the mistake of not believing Brüning, and turning a blind eye to the formidable evidence assembled during his tottering régime—have cost us dear.

*Here are a few significant tables of figures which show how, since the triumphant emergence of Hitler's Germany, the increasing peril of war has strained, and must continue to strain, the resources of British citizens of all classes, both in business and in their family budgets.*

**Income Tax**

| Rate in the £ | |
|---|---|
| 1934-5 | 4/6 |
| 1935-6 | 4/9 |
| 1936-7 | 5/- |
| 1938-9 | 5/6 |

**Retail Food Prices**

| | 1932 | 1938 |
|---|---|---|
| Bread (4 lb.) | 7d | 9½d |
| Milk (quart) | 6d | 6¾d |
| Tea (1 lb.) | 1/8¼ | 2/2½ |
| Bacon (Streaky) | 9¾d | 1/1¾ |

**Cost of Living**

(Ministry of Labour Statistics)

| | 1932 | 1938 |
|---|---|---|
| | Above 1914 | Above 1914 |
| All items | 46% | 56% |
| Food only | 29% | 40% |

LILLIPUT

## Army, Navy and Air Force

| | | | | |
|---|---|---|---|---|
| 1932–33 | ... | ... | ... | £102,990,000 |
| 1933–34 | ... | ... | ... | £107,872,000 |
| 1934–35 | ... | ... | ... | £113,869,000 |
| 1935–36 | ... | ... | ... | £137,396,000 |
| 1936–37 | ... | ... | ... | £158,211,000 |
| 1937–38 (estimates) | ... | | ... | £278,250,000 |
| 1938–39 (estimates) | ... | | ... | £343,250,000 |
| 1937–42. Special rearmament expenditure of | | | ... ... | £1,500,000,000 |

## Air Raid Precautions

| | | |
|---|---|---|
| 1936 | ... ... | £1,358,250 |
| 1937 | ... ... | £5,525,000 |
| 1938 | ... ... | £8,500,000 |

Total expenditure in next three or four years ... £32,000,000

## National Defence Contribution

This tax is payable by concerns whose profits exceed £2,000 a year

Minimum for present financial year ... £2,000,000

For next five years, per annum ... £25,000,000

## National Debt

| | | |
|---|---|---|
| 1931 | ... | £7,413,000,000 |
| 1937 | ... | £7,797,000,000 |

By Lt. R. M. Smyth

# Winston Churchill— Soldier

Wadi Halfa, 1898.

" I FIND I have got an addition to my troop, Winston Churchill, of the 4th Hussars. He's Lord Randolph's son and has been fighting in Cuba; he also took part in the Chitral campaign, about which he wrote a book; and perhaps for that reason Kitchener began by refusing to have him! He arrived, however, the night before we started, and taught us a new game called Bridge, which comes from Constantinople, and is like whist but more of a gamble. At present as I said, he is attached to my troop, but when we arrive at the place of concentration and form a fourth squadron he'll be given a troop in that. He rides with me sometimes on the march and is such good company. Keeps one awake, which is a great thing, for starting so early and going to bed so late one is apt to sleep in the saddle . . ."

" . . . Winston Churchill is only twenty-three and frightfully keen. He started by telling me he was more interested in men than horses, so I asked him to look after their rations, etc., and said I would do the horses. He asked to see the men, spoke to them (very well, too) and had a great success; in fact they liked him . . ."

" . . . I shall be very sorry when Winston Churchill leaves my troop. He is aggressively clever and bumptious, but you can't help liking him in spite of his very apparent but superficial faults. If ever you come across him get to know him; I know you'd delight in him. As specimen of his utterances, he said that in his opinion Gray's Elegy was a beautiful poem, and 'that there was not a word in it he would care to alter'; also that he did not mean, or wish, to stay in the Army, not caring to spend his life 'in the company of intelligent animals'! Of course he's very young and knows it. But if he lives he'll be a big man some day. . . ."

L.N.A.

LONDON

*Lieutenant Churchill*

27

WIDE WORLD

LONDON

*"Magic mirror on the wall who
is the fairest of them all?"*
The ex-Crown Prince of Germany

G.F.                                                                    NEW YORK

*The fairest of them all*

29

SCHALL PARIS

*Dr. Goebbels in his home*

*Lemur monkey with her young*

*" Everything for the Führer!"*
*German conscripts*

*"What do they mean?"*
*Adolf Hitler*

KEYSTONE

LOND

*Jews*
*On their way to a demonstration*

TONE
LONDON

*Baiters*
*In the foreground, Streicher, German Anti–Semite No. 1*

*"Hang it, let's declare war and get the damn thing over."*

**By Arnold Zweig**

# Return of the Gas Mask

*Arnold Zweig, author of the famous German war book "The Case of Sergeant Grischa," was in London on a visit during the crisis. In this short story, specially written for Lilliput, he describes his feelings— the feelings of a true democrat and a hater of war.*

THERE was a knock on the door. He had already gone to bed, tired from the excitement of the day, the day of that crisis which had suddenly and threateningly risen over Europe like a water-spout.

Unfortunately, his polite host said, he would have to get up to be fitted for his gas mask.

In the sitting-room two girls in brown overcoats were waiting, and a tall young man with a kindly smile. The man, 45 years old, medium height, a grey dressing-gown over his pyjamas, had not quite grasped the meaning of it all when he found himself seated in a chair, a gas-mask on his face, drawing in his breath.

One of the girls pressed a sheet of cardboard against the respirator and at once the mask sucked itself to his face, collapsing like a paper-bag from which the air has escaped. The girls uttered sounds of satisfaction : the mask fitted well, there was no leakage. Gladly and politely, it was passed to him. Not even the glasses he was wearing had proved an obstacle.

Back in his room, the man put the mask on the mantelpiece and sat down on the edge of his bed, trembling. He looked at it : after twenty years it had come back, grey, made of rubber, with a big transparent shield, very useful. Slowly and heavily his heart was beating. For all he cared it need not have returned. He did not want it.

He lay down again, put out the light and tried to sleep. It was impossible.

Suddenly in his imagination he saw the dug-out again, an awning before the entrance. Again he lay, one of a million soldiers, on his straw-mattress, feet covered with heavy boots, puttees and breeches messy with Flanders mud. Instead of the dull vibration of the bedroom windows as the wind pressed against them, he heard the rolling of drumfire about a mile away.

It was unbearable.

He got up. The electric light flooded his peaceful yellow room, light which would have sufficed for three dug-outs. He dressed, took hat and rain-coat, and went out. The street lay empty under shining lamps, and the September wind played with the leaves which fell from the trees like spent cartridges from the chambers of a rifle.

Hands deep in his pockets, the man trudged to a main road and jumped on a bus. After a penny ride he got off again, and turning into the first side-street, marched on. He took the wrong turning without noticing it. Everything round him seemed changed. The pointed gables did not look like London any more, but like those of a town in the north of France—like Amiens or one of the small towns near there.

Cold wrath shook him. It had all been in vain. All the misery, all the toil, the immense efforts, the bitterness about the unnecessary, blind slaughter. The running under shell-fire, dropping down, jumping up again, the thrust of the bayonet into bodies, soft and resisting, of other men, the running back, the trembling and crouching in shell-holes, the wild fling of the hand-grenade at the last moment. All in vain. They had come back again, the steel-helmets—those obedient idiots, who had forced him too to wear a hat of steel instead of comfortable felt for all those years.

Twenty years, the better part of his manhood had been wiped out.

The street ended in an open square with a lawn and trees. He realized at once where he was. By the light of the high lamps he saw a group of men digging : they were digging a trench.

Some of the trees he had loved had already been cut down. In their place the smooth steel neck of an anti-aircraft gun was pointing to the clouds, threatening and searching, like a boy's air-gun aiming at sparrows. The "sparrows" were not there yet, but oh! they would turn up all right.

He stood near them, in the full light, so that he could not be mistaken for a spy. The digging men were in high spirits ; apparently they had been out of work for a long time.

The man, hands in his pockets, thought. How had it been possible for everything to come back ? Had it not been well buried on the

eleventh of November, 1918 ? Had
they not pushed their bayonets into
the ground, spat and said that
a better time was coming now ?
He felt for his pipe in his pocket and,
hardly conscious of what he was
doing, stood against the wind,
sheltering his face with his hat, and
lit it. It was still half-filled with
good English shag.

Over in Ireland he had a young
wife whom he loved, and two little
girls. It was better like that. At
least one knew for whom one took
up a rifle and carried hand-grenades,
if things started again.

It must not start again. Why the
hell should it! All because of those
foreign scoundrels who never could
get enough land and subjects and
prestige.

He did not want prestige. He
loved his family, his work, the
stamps he was already collecting

for his girls, for Lilian and Ruth. And back there in his room on the mantelpiece stood the gas mask, and through its big window grinned at him and his impotent wishes.

He saw it before him as if it filled the whole sky, which was also dark-grey, with a pale glimmering cloud instead of the shield.

It was not his fault that it had come so far. He was a victim of those people who made politics their business, as he made selling paper his. But they knew less about their business than he knew about his. They now had to declare themselves bankrupt.

While he was standing thus, feeling the trunk of a tree between his shoulders like another spine, a thought began slowly to take possession of him, rising from that part of his stomach where he used to wear his cartridge pouches. It travelled through his throat, choking him, it left a bitter taste in his mouth and pressed against his skull.

No, no, he did not want it to be true. But it was true, the thought that told him: it was his fault too.

Undoubtedly and fundamentally. He could not complain. He had left it to the others to carry on what they believed to be the right

politics, he had not bothered much about it, had forgotten his experiences and permitted those others to believe that they were dealing with the decent Germans. And meanwhile the huns had reappeared, marching in rows upon the Germans, drilling them for war.

Like 1917. Like 1918. The eleventh of November was still a long way off. Was there still time to acquire truth?

One of the workmen dropped his spade and wiped the sweat from his face. The man approached him and took off his coat, saying—as he would have said to an exhausted comrade in the trenches—"My turn now, mate, let me do my bit now." The man, astonished, took advantage of the offer to go into the shade for a moment.

The man thrust his spade into the earth with a swing—all his muscles seemed to remember the movement. And while he did so, he decided that from now on he would watch the machinations of his rulers as intently, with distrust in his eyes, as he was now watching the ground, as if the enemy were lying hidden behind it.

Let the gas-mask grin on the mantelpiece. He had been roused for good. Now he could go home to bed.

*"I'm sorry Madam, they're all one shade, greyey-black, with off-white canvas straps . . ."*

*"Lady Cornchester's car!"*

# WARNING

## PROBLEMS OF TO-DAY

# A.R.P.

## By John Langdon-Davies

I BELIEVE that those of us who desire peace above all else would do well to regard A.R.P. as our most important practical concern during 1939.

Modern war has become so destructive and so costly that only a nation prepared to gamble on a short war will be likely to break the peace. Everywhere the doors are barred by Maginot Lines ; it is only the windows that are still open. The God of War must fly in through them.

The greatest temptation to the predatory powers who have been practising air banditry on the prostrate Spanish people is the lack of preparedness against air attack of Britain. We are the most vulnerable of nations because we are so highly developed industrially and because our chief city is not a city at all but a tract of land flooded with people. As things are, it is a real temptation to Hitler to launch an attack against a target like London, which cannot be missed.

Let us not waste time asking why official A.R.P. has so far been farci-

cal; let us bury gas-proof rooms and gas masks in oblivion. What are the essentials of A.R.P. as the experience of Barcelona and common-sense alike reveal them ?

If we are to become A.R.P.-minded, we must realise that the peace-time life to which we have become reconciled must be altered fundamentally. Real A.R.P. does not mean digging a large number of shelters and then going on living as we have done heretofore. It means altering our cities and our way of living in them so that at a moment's notice they may become part of the front line trenches in a war thrust upon us by the air bandits of international Fascism.

Fortunately, we can solve A.R.P. only by solving peace-time problems which ought to have been settled long ago. In broad outline this is what we must do :

1. We must solve our traffic problems. One of the chief objects of air bombardment is to make civilian life impossible by bringing it to a standstill.

43

London is particularly vulnerable; fifty well-placed bombs would immobilise it. Anyone who has tried to get out of London for a Bank Holiday week-end will know that this is so.

Unless we make London a city of rapid transit and easy exit we are doomed. London to-day is like a huge theatre without emergency doors ; if a fire comes there will be trouble.

Traffic should be sent underground far more scientifically than it is at present. In war time all surface traffic will be dangerous. Underground tubes, probably on the Kearney plan, are the only solution.

2. We must solve our problems of urban congestion. At present London and many other cities are fire traps. Incendiary bombs would wreck certain districts inevitably. The only solution is wholesale demolition without rebuilding. Instead of new flats we need space. The modern city, that is, the city for which A.R.P. can be planned, must be an open city, a combination of country and town.

3. Only when we have accepted this large-scale remodelling of our cities as essential, can we begin to make sense of A.R.P. And we must begin by realising that A.R.P. is a psychological problem far more than a structural or technical one.

The object of air bombardment is not to hit military objectives but to attack the nerve centres of the man in the street. We must prepare our defence now by letting everybody know exactly what to expect from an air raid and by training them to withstand the nervous shock such a raid entails.

Apathy is a curse, but so is defeatism. It is quite possible to experience an air raid with equanimity, but only if one is mentally trained to do so.

The key to the psychological factor is that everyone must have work to do during an air raid. Then the siren does not become a signal of alarm but a call to action. People prepare to be useful, not to be frightened.

4. A.R.P. depends above all on adequate warning. There must be five minutes warning and there must be no false alarms. The worst raid in Spanish history, against Granollers, owed its success to failure of the warning system. False alarms are as dangerous, as they immobilise the population and in time make them careless.

Air raid warnings should be much more than a mere system of sirens. Wireless should take a part, to

*"Get ready—6–44—Steady—6–45—6–46, Go!"*

instruct, to reassure, to explain. Left to themselves, people imagine that the danger is greater than it is. Wireless should explain what is happening, above all teach men to distinguish between "our" anti-aircraft guns and their bombs. This gives greater confidence.

5. There must be shelter for those who have to work in dangerous areas. I do not believe that everyone can be protected against a thousand-pound bomb, but much more should be done than has as yet been attempted. Every factory, every office should be provided with bomb-proof refuges, or people upon whom our economic life depends will not be able to carry on work.

So far as deep shelters are provided, they must be connected with underground roads or tubes. If all London sat still sixty feet underground for three weeks, the war would be lost even if there were no casualties. We must never forget that the defence must not merely keep alive, it must keep working.

6. Above all, there must be adequate, perfectly thought out evacuation schemes. These must not merely be billeting plans for children. Huge populations must be shifted. London must be transformed. The East End must invade the West End and the West End go elsewhere. And it must all be thought out *now*. *Then* will be too late.

Now that is the barest outline of what A.R.P. means. Have we gone any distance towards achieving it?

We have barely begun.

Gas masks? Gas-proof rooms? Nonsense : springes to catch woodcocks.

For real air warfare London is as unprepared as Barcelona was at the beginning of the Spanish war, in spite of the lessons we could have learned from Spain.

"O.K., then; we'll dismiss the idea of a reinforced concrete ceiling
over the whole of London. It was only a preliminary suggestion . . ."

## By Daniel Defoe

## Plague of London

*Orders published by the Lord Mayor and Aldermen of the City of London concerning the Infection of the Plague* 1665.

IT is now upon special consideration thought very expedient for preventing and avoiding of sickness that these officers following be appointed and these orders duly observed. In every Parish . . . examiners . . . to continue two months at least . . . to every infected house two watchmen. Women searchers in every Parish.

\*　　\*　　\*

That the Constables see every house shut up and to be attended with watchmen and every house visited be marked with a red Cross of a foot long evident to be seen.

That no staffs, bedding or garments be suffered.to be carried or conveyed out of an infected house.

\*　　\*　　\*

That no dogs or cats or tame pigeons or ponies be suffered to be kept within any part of the city, or any swine to be in the streets or lanes but that such swine be impounded by the beadle.

\*　　\*　　\*

None shall be removed out of the house where he falleth sick of the infection into any other house except it be to the Pest House (hospital) or a tent or into some such house which the owner of the visited house holdeth in his own hands.

## By Sir John Anderson

# A.R.P.

*The Protection of Your Home against Air Raids. Home Office Pamphlet.* 1940.

IF air raids ever come to this country . . . do not hesitate to ask for advice if you need it. A local Air Raid Precautions organisation has been established in your district and Air Raid Wardens have been appointed to help you. For any help you need, apply to your Warden or to your local Council Offices.

\* \* \*

All windows, skylights, glazed doors or other openings in parts of the house where lights are used must be completely screened after dusk so that no light is visible from outside. All lights near an outside door must be screened.

Clear the loft, attic or top floor of all inflammable material—paper, litter, lumber, etc.—to lessen the danger of fire and prevent fire from spreading.

\* \* \*

If you live in a large town think whether you can make arrangements for pets to be sent away the moment danger threatens. Animals will help to use up the supply of air in a room. Count two dogs or cats as one person in choosing the size of your refuge room.

\* \* \*

Wounded and gas-contaminated casualties who can should walk direct to the nearest First-aid Post. Remove the affected garment, then wash yourself immediately. Stretcher cases will be taken immediately to hospital.

# OPPORTUNITY

# What They Say About the Black-Out

**Husband:**

This black-out's going to cause a lot of trouble. I asked if I could see her home before I realised that I'd bumped into my own wife.

**Wife:**

He came in with powder on his lapels, and said he'd tripped over some sandbags. Well, I've never heard of whitewash that smells of chypre.

**Harriet:**

'E said 'Didn't you see my luminous button?' I let 'im 'ave it, *properly* luminous, I was.

**Harry:**

I used to do a nice trade with the fruit barrow after the lamps was lit. What I say at black-out time ain't fit for nobody's ears—barrin' 'Itler's.

**Psychologist:**

These nights provide interesting contrasts in reflex action. My observations indicate that the impact of a body of the opposite sex causes 27 per cent. of females to exclaim, 11 per cent. to giggle, 9 per cent. to swear, 2 per cent. to run, and 51 per cent. to cling.

**Snob:**

It was my fault that I knocked the man off the kerb. But what annoys me is that I'd apologised before I realised he was only a workman.

**Social Worker:**

The increasing numbers of young couples in our parks is a most regrettable feature of the black-out. I won't dwell on details, but every flash of my torch reveals some degree of looseness.

**Poet:**

I was composing the opening —'*The soul sheds rays upon the path obscure*'—when a bicycle caught me sideways and both the rider and the second line escaped me.

**Schoolgirl:**

If only they'd let me go out in the evening I'd have a chance of being taken for years older.

**Schoolboy:**

This is the game. We each have a banana skin and choose a bit of pavement. The first who bags a victim wins. If they just skid it doesn't score.

**Dance Hostess:**

They used to drive me back to Maida Vale on the chance of being asked in. But now they as good as ask 'Are you going to make it worth my petrol?'

**Film Star:**

I arrived at midnight and said I guessed I could only guess the policemen were wonderful . . .

**Lady:**

My precious Fido can't even glimpse the lamp posts. But the darling's *so* intelligent, he still finds them.

**Gay Girl:**

We were heading for Delvano's and found ourselves screeching with boredom in the Purple Pig. Why doesn't the government or someone do something about everything?

**Charlady:**

For six months I've been treatin' my next-door very 'aughty, and now it's all so much time wasted, because last night I answered 'er as pleasant as you please, before I spotted 'oo it was.

**Landlady:**

She said he was an A.R.P. warden, and he'd called about her light. They switched it off and I knocked on the door and said he'd got to go, if he'd quite finished with his precautions.

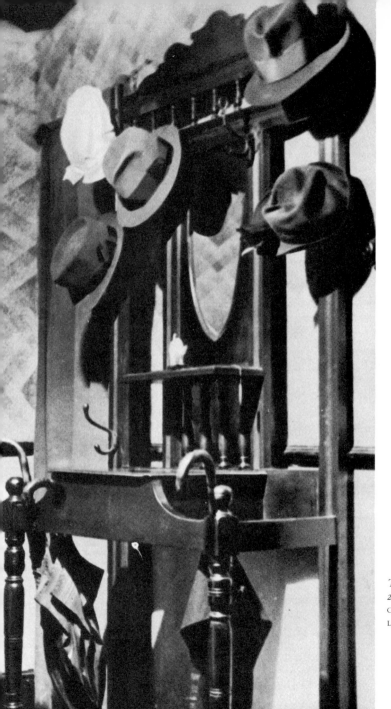

*This was on
27th September, 1938*
CHADDOCK
LIVERPOOL

*And this was on
1st October, 1938*
CHADDOCK
LIVERPOOL

LISA
WELW

*Newly hatched chick*

LONDON

*Air-raid warden*

CENTRAL PRESS

LOND

*"Was that an air raid warning?"*
*London Statue*

YSTONE LONDON

*"Don't worry, we're ready for them"*
*Chadwell Heath A.R.P. Post*

GIDAL                                                                    LONDC

*Cactus needs no care*

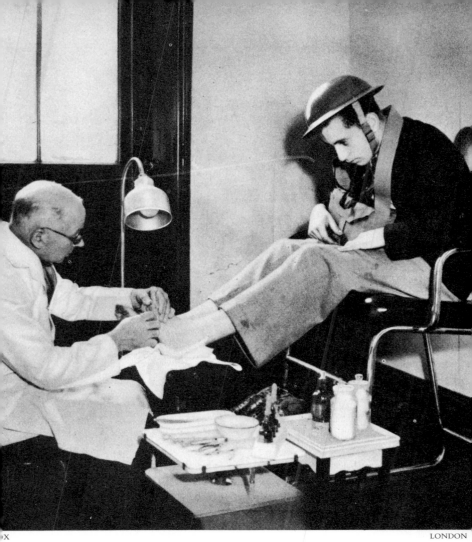

X

*Warden's feet need attention*

# EVACUEES

## From the Notebook of a Billeting Officer

I'M sorry, we can't take a child; my husband keeps his fishing tackle in the spare room.

**No, the maids would give notice at once.**

I'm afraid not. You see my wife's

expecting a happy event quite soon.

**I know it looks as if we have room, but mother** has only just left, and my aunts are due any day now.

Only if she's a Theosophist.

**No. My husband disapproves of the whole idea of evacuation.** I can't manage if she's any fancy religion.

**We are reserved for officers.**

I'll only take her if she's got no parents.

**Yes, if she is a hard worker, a neat seamstress, a good cook and quick on her feet.**

Well, we're sleeping five in the kitchen now, but if you can find a corner to fit them in, you're welcome . . .

**The doctor says my nerves couldn't possibly stand it . . .**

Frankly I can't be bothered.

**Sorry, sir, but what with my husband's snoring, it just wouldn't be fair on the kid.**

Certainly not. My house is nicely furnished.

**My husband has got a much better scheme. He keeps writing to the papers about it.**

I'll take her, but it must be clearly understood that the dogs come first.

**Not a London child. The things we've heard about London children . . .**

I'm sorry, but I just can't do with the War at all.

**Who is it, dear? The Billeting Officer. Well, say mother's out...**

Certainly. I can't help feeling it might be my little Doris in need of a home.

*"I got fed up with Canada, Ma."*

# Lord Rothermere

This is what Lord Rothermere says about Hitler in his boo[k]
himself a man of the people but, notwithstanding, the impres[sion]
that of a great gentleman (page 136). There is no man living who
soon[...]

## This is what Hitler Says

The German Government will scrupulously respect every treaty voluntar[ily]
signed, even if concluded before its entry into power. It will therefore in particul[ar]
respect and fulfil all obligations arising from the Locarno Pact.

**May 21, 1935**

The German Government will unconditionally respect all other clauses of t[he]
Versailles Treaty, including the territorial clauses.

**May 21, 1935**

The assertion that the Reich intends to overpower the Austrian State is absu[rd]
and can by no means be proved or substantiated.

**January 30, 1934**

Germany neither intends nor wishes to interfere in the internal affairs [of]
Austria, to annex Austria or to conclude an Anschluss.

**May 21, 1935**

No people desires peace more than the German people. Germany only wishe[s]
to live and work in peace and quiet.

**March 12, 1936**

We are ready to conclude a non-aggression pact with Czechoslovakia.

**March 7, 1936**

We have no territorial demands to make in Europe.

**March 7, 1936**

This is the last territorial claim I have to make in Europe. I have assure[d]
Mr. Chamberlain, and I emphasise it now, that when this problem is solve[d]
Germany has no more territorial problems in Europe. When the Czechs sha[ll]
have come to an understanding with their other minorities, I shall not be intereste[d]
in the Czech State any more.

**September 26, 1938**

# s Always Right

*nings and Predictions* : "... Herr Hitler is proud to call
*hat* has remained with me after every meeting with him is
*hise* given in regard to something of real moment I would
..." (page 135).

## And this is what Hitler Does

*ermany unilaterally denounced the Locarno Treaty, which her Government*
*voluntarily accepted and which had not been infringed by any other signatory*
*er.*

**March 7, 1936**

*erman troops reoccupied the demilitarised portion of the Rhineland, in viola-*
*of the Treaty of Versailles and the Treaty of Locarno.*

**March 7, 1936**

*Nazi rising in Austria planned by Germany. Austrian Nazis mustered in*
*man territory ready for invasion. Chancellor Dollfuss assassinated in Vienna.*

**July 25, 1934**

*Austrian Chancellor Schuschnigg forced to resign by threat of German invasion.*
*man troops invaded Austria. Austria annexed.*

**March, 1938**

*German troops and aircraft sent to Spain to take part in Civil War. German*
*es bomb Spanish towns, killing civilians.*

**1936-1939**

*German ultimatum to Czechoslovakia to cede Sudeten areas or be invaded.*

**September, 1938**

*udeten areas of Czechoslovakia annexed after Munich.*
**October, 1938**

*lovakia encouraged to separate from Czechoslovakia.*
*ohemia and Moravia invaded by large German army. Czech Government*
*d to capitulate under threat of bombardment of Prague. Prague occupied.*
*h State annexed.*
*Memel annexed after ultimatum to Lithuania.*

**March, 1939**

# HYPOCRISY

by Frederick the Great

## Protector, 1756

*Frederick the Great's statement of 1756, made to the army and announcing the invasion of Poland which launched the Seven Years' War*

"THE iniquitous designs of the Court of Vienna place the King under the necessity of anticipating an enemy who most emphatically rejects offers of conciliation.

"Despite His wishes, His Majesty sees Himself forced to enter, with His army, into the hereditary Estates of the King of Poland, Elector of Saxony.

"It is with regret that the King finds Himself obliged to undertake measures which His personal friendship for His Polish Majesty would have made Him avoid, did not the rules of war, the ill-fortune of the times, and the security of His own Estates render such action indispensable.

"Everybody knows of the consideration which His Majesty has exercised in his relations with the Court of Saxony, and of the baleful consequences resulting from it; . . . the union of its forces with those of his enemies, and finally the dangerous plot to attack the King in the very centre of his Estates.

"Under these same circumstances the King feels compelled to consult but the dictates of prudence.

"In adopting His policy His Majesty declares most categorically and in the face of all Europe that He does not enter as an enemy; but solely for reasons of security; that He will make His troops observe the strictest discipline and that, compelled to give way to the most urgent considerations, He will only await the happy moment when these same considerations shall permit Him to extend to this Prince an undertaking which shall always remain sacred with Him."

# DECEIT

## by Adolf Hitler

# Benefactor, 1939

*Adolf Hitler's message to the Services and speech to the Reichstag, delivered September 2nd, 1939, announcing the invasion of Poland which launched the second World War*

"THE Polish State has refused the peaceful settlement of relations which I desired and has appealed to arms.

"Germany was prepared to settle the questions of Danzig and of the Corridor by the method of negotiation on the basis of a proposal of truly unparalleled magnanimity.

"A series of violations of the frontier, intolerable to a great Power, prove that Poland is no longer willing to respect the frontier of the Reich. In order to put an end to this lunacy, I have no other

Trier

choice than to meet force with force.

"I am determined to see to it that a change is made in the relationship between Germany and Poland that shall ensure a peaceful co-existence. In this I am resolved to continue to fight until either the present Polish Government is willing to bring about this change or until another Polish Government is ready to do so.

"I am resolved to remove from the German frontier the element of uncertainty, the everlasting atmosphere of conditions resembling civil war.

"I will see to it that in the East there is, on the frontier, a peace, precisely similar to that on our other frontiers.

"I will take the necessary measures to see that they do not contradict the proposals I have already made known in the Reichstag itself, to the rest of the world, that is to say, I will not war against women and children.

"I have ordered my Air Force to restrict itself to attacks on military objectives . . ."

KEYSTONE

*Guardsmen*

LON

*Prime minister*

PLANET NEWS

LONI

*The man who lost his appeasement*
*Neville Chamberlain*

STONE

LONDON

*"Heavens, I forgot to occupy the United States
what will the Führer say?"*
*German Foreign Secretary von Ribbentrop*

69

*Success*

*Failure*

GOHLER

LON

*Bulldog breed*

*Winston Churchill*

*"If I say you're Hitler, you're Hitler, see?"*

**By Osbert Sitwell**

# Send the Public Schools to Germany

EACH of us, I suspect, cherishes secretly and far down within himself his own war aims, in addition to the declared national ends of beating the enemy and building up a better world. Some find solace in their dreams of Federal Union, some in a world made fit for Esperanto: others possess, like myself, their own ambitions, but as yet unavowed.

In a book of essays published some years ago, Bertrand Russell pointed out that every man you meet seems to be happy in strict proportion to the eccentricity of the beliefs he cherishes. He who elects to believe in a flat earth, or that Shakespeare wrote Tennyson's poems—or Tennyson, Shakespeare's—spends every moment of his existence here below in happy delirium.

Similarly my private peace aim, which I now bring boldly into the open, is to transfer—nay, compulsorily to deport — our public schools to Germany. Their need is greater than ours.

Eton I should build outside Potsdam, and Harrow should blossom in Charlottenburg; Winchester should cultivate its notions in Worms and Fettes tame its doric types in Dresden. For I believe that the English Public School System alone can save Germany from itself, and so the world from Germany.

The average boy, whether Nordic, Mediterranean or Alpine, is at heart when in a herd—not individually—a bully; the English Public School System ensures that at some period of his career the bully shall be bullied. A good English public school is a more comfortable form of concentration camp: the same discipline, only milder; the same dependence on physical exercise; the same horror of the unusual and of the things of the mind, prevail. It acts, therefore, as a kind of inoculation against the concentration-camp spirit. In after life, a man who has endured all its horrors—the food, the floggings, the compulsory attendance at chapel, the jokes of the masters—will defend his freedom with all his might.

The great fear, the phobia, the secret, unspoken at the back of the mind—if such it can be called —of every ex-public-school boy is that, after the manner of Mr. Bultitude (in that epic of the national subconscious, *"Vice Versa"*), he may wake up to find himself once more at school! Introduce that terror into German hearts, and you may live to see a free Germany and a free world.

Moreover, by the time he leaves school, the boy from an English public school has learnt to disbelieve in the beliefs that have been so carefully instilled in him. He knows—and this, though slight in itself, is on the positive as opposed to the negative side— that personal style, even if rebellious, should be more highly esteemed than sycophancy, and that a great deal is forgiven, and should be forgiven, to those who sin in a gentle and genial way. He recognises—and in such a comprehension the very essence of civilisation resides—that the exceptions to his own standards are sometimes more worthy than the whole body of those who conform to them. But the exception, he understands, must be exceptional; it must be a Nelson, and not an ordinary man, who

puts his blind eye to the telescope, a Wellington to run away from his first battle.

The Etonian knows, even if he does not know why, that Shelley and Swinburne, and a hundred such others, constitute the glory of his school: but the German does not realise even yet that the Germans who transgressed the German code, from Heine to Thomas Mann, are part of the glory of the human race.

But so far, like the public school itself, we have neglected education. The masters of the English public schools, by boring the boys interned under their care, unconsciously inculcate in them a healthy dislike of mental effort, while consciously they inculcate (and this is just as valuable) a horror of modern science. No lazy man—that is, no man turned out by a public school—has ever much harmed the world, still less brought ruin on it. No man has ever much injured his fellow men by liking to play that drowsy game cricket, by a fondness for hot baths or good food.

No, such were not the habits of Attila, of Jenghiz Khan or the blessed Karl Marx, any more than they to-day constitute the recreations of Hitler or Dr. Goebbels. Let us remember, as we send our schools to Germany, that no slothful man has ever invented, or tried to invent, dynamite or incendiary bomb or death ray. It is the active man, with the active mind, who does the harm. Eschew the energetic, and especially him, who, for the sake of being able to work still harder—and so, of doing still more harm—lives on milk and vegetables. If only Hitler and Goebbels had been sent to a good English public school, how different life would be to-day, for both English and Germans! But, as they did not go, we must send the public schools out to them and see that the next generation of Germans, at any rate, is educated there.

Thus the future German citizen, if the English Public School System came to his help, would grow up to prefer dead languages and dead processes of thought to those that are alive. It would, too, teach him (with my public-school education, I had almost written "learn him"!) to prefer the wars of Cæsar to those of Frederick the Great or Bismarck, and to prefer football before all. A classical education on the English model would also induce him, without his being conscious of this tendency, to take the side of the Romans against the barbarian German, Belgian and British tribes, and thus to become a partisan of civilisation. It would persuade him that boxing came before duelling. Gradually, he would grow to recognise that stealing civilised European countries that are too weak and small to oppose you "isn't cricket."

If Europe is to survive, Germany must learn to relax; and that is what the English Public School System can achieve, if transplanted, while at the same time ridding ourselves of a tyranny: for us unnecessary and outgrown.

*"Now don't you go looking at the end first."*

**By Erwin Blumenfeld**

# How I Won the Iron Cross

**D**URING the World War—the last one—I had the honour of spending part of my youth as a German ambulance driver on the Western front. And there it was I won the Iron Cross.

At that time (things are different now) I was still too young to be brave. I was only 18.

One day as we were resting peacefully, the Corporal called me: "Blumenfeld," he said, "you're a brainy fellow, you know French. In a month's time I shall be going on leave, and by then I must know French perfectly. Perfectly, do you understand? If you can teach me perfect French in one month, I'll give you the Iron Cross."

"First or Second Class?" I inquired.

At that he became angry, and shouted: "I could order you to teach me French if I wanted to! But you'll obey me even without orders, do you understand?"

"Yes, Corporal."

I realised that I shouldn't be able to get anything more in the way of decorations out of him, so I asked whether, in view of the exhausting brain work these lessons would entail, I might stay in bed until nine in the morning.

This permission was granted.

The next morning at 10 I reported to the Corporal. I did not possess a French grammar, but I happened at that time to be reading Stendhal's "Le Rouge Et Le Noir." I took this book along with me and explained respectfully to the Corporal that the first thing he must do was accustom his tongue and his ear to the sound of French vowels. For this purpose, I told him, he must learn the whole of Stendhal's "Le Rouge Et Le Noir" by heart.

I read aloud very slowly:—"La petite ville de Verrières peut passer pour l'une des plus jolies de la Franche-Comté."

The Corporal repeated this five hundred times. A week later, with a little assistance from me, he was almost word perfect.

I then went on to the second sentence: "Ses maisons blanches, avec leurs toits pointus de tuiles

*"Just look at him, my dear! BLACK tie with TAILS!"*

rouges, s'étendent sur la pente d'une colline, dont des touffes de vigoureux chataigniers marquent les moindres sinuosités."

Inspired Stendhal! This sentence was too much for my Corporal. He shouted, he stuttered, I saw tears in his eyes. He spluttered, he fought, he struggled. But he never succeeded in memorising even the first ten words.

A week later I was summoned to the orderly room.

"Blumenfeld," said the Corporal, "I've had enough of you and your French lessons. I shan't need you any more."

"But what about my Iron Cross?"

"Your Iron Cross? Well . . . I'm a man of my word. You shall have your Iron Cross."

"First Class? With the black and white ribbon?"

"Yes, blast you, with the black and white ribbon. Now get out."

I left the room. I was a hero. I had won the Iron Cross.

And nowadays, whenever I look at a photograph of Herr Hitler proudly wearing the Iron Cross on his breast, I think: "I wonder how he won his? I know he can't speak French."

*The man who won the Iron Cross. Erwin Blumenfeld, famous photographer of women, who describes on the previous pages how he became a German war-hero*

# The Young Man Nobody Wanted

EARLY in the summer of 1913 a young student of technology from Vienna rented a room in the station quarter of Munich. The landlady told him that she had had to put out the former lodger because he had not paid his rent for a long time. During this conversation the poor dismissed lodger came in; he, too, was an Austrian. He took courage and asked his compatriot for permission to spend at least one more night in his room—on the sofa. The new lodger was good-hearted, took the poor devil out for a glass of beer, and they arranged that for the present he should sleep on the sofa until he should have money enough to pay for his share of the room. The two remained room-mates for over a year; the young engineer from Vienna and his guest on the sofa, the designer of advertisements from Linz.

The designer was without friends. He avoided contact with women almost fanatically; he had none of the gaiety of youth. With his insistent seriousness, he oppressed and embittered the mood of others. His room-mate, who enjoyed life, had several girl friends, and wanted to saddle his friend with one of them for Sunday. His friend exploded and rejected the proposition in no uncertain terms, flinging violent reproaches at his astonished friend: it wasn't right to turn the poor girls' heads, they took it all seriously, and afterwards felt betrayed.

He had no girl friends, but no men friends either. Neither he nor others mention any closer human relationship; later, in fact, he even boasted of having been so lonely that no one bothered about him at all. He was unfit to be a human being. . . .

. . . On August 1, 1914 a mass overpowered by enthusiasm stood in front of the ornate Feldherrn Halle and listened to the reading of a proclamation announcing the declaration of war. At a window stood a photographer. Ten or twelve years later, this photographer ran across one of the pictures taken on this occasion and published it. Among the many hundred heads he discovered a face which, despite the conspicuous ordinariness of his features, seemed illumined by an emotion unusual even in this crowd. It was a haggard, sickly face; the broad, bushy moustache gave it an artificially wild look; the protruding hyperthyroid eyes sent forth an exaggerated gleam, as though the face were addressing someone in Heaven and saying: Take notice of me, O Lord!

*Who was the mysterious lodger? Whose is that anonymous misogynistic back? See page 238.*

*"Owing to the international situation the match with
St. Trinian's has been postponed"*

# TRIUMPH

By P. L. Farago

# Father of Air Raids

YOU probably think that the inventive genius of our century is responsible for that highly progressive method of extinguishing human lives—aerial bombardment. But you are wrong. As far back as 1849, a handful of pioneers had reached this important milestone of civilisation.

In the spring of 1849, during the fighting between Italy and Austria, a young officer in the Austrian army, Uchatius by name, evolved a plan for bombing Venice from the air. This fired the imagination of the Austrian staff and they instructed Uchatius and his brother to carry out experiments.

The two brothers soon began their experiments with "Montgolfier" balloons, filled with hot air. For weeks they studied air currents and built balloons. The result was a paper contraption capable of carrying a 20-pound bomb for about 30 minutes.

Experiments having proved successful, our pioneers presented their government with a list of details and costs, probably the first air budget in history. The items were: 100 "Montgolfier" balloons, 50 stoves to heat the air, and 100 bombs. The budget was sent to the Emperor himself. In gracious consideration of the noble cause, he consented to it.

In the summer, Uchatius carried out his plan. He was given a battleship for an operating base. He first released a trial balloon, and then, having found the right direction, sent off the balloons, each fitted with a bomb and an apparatus for releasing it at the right time.

Most of the bombs fell in the wrong places, and the raid therefore did not cause much material damage in Venice; but its moral effect upon the population was tremendous.

The inventor was urged to repeat the raid. He did so, but the whole thing proved to be rather ineffective: only 4 people were killed and 40 injured in the air raids. This did not satisfy the war chiefs, and they sent Uchatius away in disgrace.

He died in ignorance of the glorious future of his invention.

"*Next, an air–raid siren, followed by a dive bomber, and ending with a screaming bomb . . .*"

*"No privacy! No privacy!"*

## By Joseph Cotton

# Mechanic in an
# Air Raid

I WAS feeling a bit tired so I went round by the time office to look at the clock. It was five minutes to seven and I decided I would knock off at seven. I took off my overalls and hung them on a nail, opened my drawer to get my soap to have a wash. Somebody had nabbed mine so I borrowed Ron's and went down the end of the shop to the washroom.

It was quieter in here than out in the shop and the splashing of water was the only sound. I was hypnotised by the way in which the lather dropped from my hands in big dirty blobs and went swirling round and round before vanishing down the plughole. I'd go to the pictures to-night I decided.

There was a crash. Like thunder it was: like the sheet-metal thunder you hear in amateur theatricals, a thousand times magnified. The floor, concrete, was shaking. Air blasted in through the door hit me like a whip-lash. I went down on the floor close to the wall.

Paddy burst in and flopped down beside me. "It's all right, mate," he was shouting, "it's all right." A big sheet of plywood fell from above and landed beside us, we pulled it up over us and glass and brick beat down upon it. Crash followed crash. We could hear the whine of each bomb—every one was coming straight at us and we clung close together like a couple of kids. We were afraid—those bombs were close.

Paddy's face was close to mine, his nose was bleeding, blood running down and dripping off his chin.

"The bastards," he yelled in my ear. "The dirty German bastards."

Explosions were coming from underneath us. I was waiting for the floor to open up and hurl us skywards. There came a lapse and we lifted our heads.

Plaster dust filled the air and I could not see across to the other wall. Paddy saw the dust and yelled, "It's gas. The bastards are dropping gas." He struggled up, remained for a moment as a blurred silhouette in the doorway, then vanished from view.

The dust was down my throat, I could not breathe and wanted a drink. I crawled out from under the plywood and went over to the sinks. Falling brick had knocked the bottoms out of most of them. I put my mouth under the tap and drank. I noticed a poem pencilled on the whitewashed wall —it concerned the foreman. A piece of chewing gum was stuck there too.

I could hear the rising note of an aircraft engine and dived under the plywood once more. More explosions and whining. Crashes that made the whole scene shake like the picture thrown on a sheet by a cheap cine projector.

How lonely I felt. I wished Paddy had not gone. The dust cleared a little and I could see out through the door. I got an impression of a great crack racing diagonally across the face of a wall. It sagged, bulged, then fell like a man struck behind the knees. I could see deep blue sky and clouds where the roof had been.

Then it was quiet. I kicked the protective plywood away and sat leaning against the wall for some moments. I thought:

"How many are dead? Quite a few, I bet." The door was hanging on one hinge.

"How am I—all there? Not a scratch." A procession of people was passing the door, feet crunching on the glass-strewn floor. They nearly had cut heads from the fallen glass.

Two men went by carrying a third between them. One of his shoes had come off, there was a hole in the heel of his sock.

"Poor devil. How bloody his face is. Wonder if Ron and Moggie and the other blokes are O.K.?"

Small pieces of glass were still dropping, tinkling, to the floor, like the rain drips from trees when the storm has passed.

"Better get out."

I got up, passed out into the shop and picked my way between benches, over the floor strewn with brick and glass to where my coat hung. I slung it over my arm and walked to the other end of the shop. A bomb had landed close here. Figures were stretched out between the benches. First-aid men were passing amongst them. They lay where they had fell and the falling dust settling upon them had transformed them into so many statues and made them a part of the debris in which they lay.

There were pieces of men, too.

I went into the street. A Ford V8 was lying upside down on the wrecked roof of the building opposite. Falling telegraph poles had festooned the roofs with wire.

The road was covered with glass and brick and steel girderwork from roofs. One building was on fire and a column of black smoke rose into the blue evening sky. Firemen were on the scene and their heavy rubber boots made a clumping noise as they moved backwards and forwards getting the hoses unrolled.

People were still coming out of the stricken buildings. A group of girls came out, some of them with faces stained a shocking crimson with blood from head cuts. Some were hysterical.

Two men in shrapnel helmets carried a figure out on a stretcher and placed it near to where I was standing. It was a woman and her clothes had been blasted off. She lay very still. I wondered if she were dead. The row of silent helpless figures grew longer and cars were commandeered to get them to hospital.

I knew some of those silent figures. It could not be reality. Things like this never happen to people you know—only to persons you read of in the newspapers or see in the newsreels.

At this point the air-raid sirens blared out, tearing on nerves that had already been taxed to the utmost. I went down a ditch by the side of a factory wall. People were running in every direction. Ambulance men were trying to get a stretcher through the narrow entrance to a shelter.

Spitfires and Hurricanes roared low overhead, forming a protective circle around the stricken area. Some people saw them and just flung themselves flat, hands covering their ears. "They're our boys. It's O.K. They're ours," someone shouted.

A man walked slowly across the road and sat down on a pile of bricks, his right coat sleeve had gone and his arm was severely lacerated. A friend put a cigarette in his mouth and lit it for him. He looked up at him, smiled quietly, then drew on his cigarette and stared at the ground as he drew patterns in the dust with the toe of his shoe.

The planes had gone and it was very quiet, save for the crackling of flames. Beside me in the ditch was a heap of big cardboard boxes. Some had burst open—they contained radio sets.

There were no more bombs and the "All Clear" soon sounded. I caught sight of Ron across the road, pulling his bike out from under a pile of bricks.

"Bloody awful, wasn't it?" he said.

"Yes," I replied, "I lost your soap." We laughed—we could afford to laugh, for we had been very lucky.

## Gulliver's Diary

ON the night when one of London's best-known cafés was bombed, we were at the crowded Hungaria. Shortly after 10 p.m. numbers of dusty, and even blood-stained, people began to come in. In the men's washroom there was a Captain of Tanks scrubbing the grime from his face and hands. " Well, I'm going to finish my dinner somewhere," he said. And he did. He had struggled out of the destroyed restaurant.

Among the women having a wash and fluff up, there were two girls in dishevelled evening dresses. They, too, had come from the café. They were calmly preparing for another two hours of dancing, but they had a dog with them—a fox terrier—and he stood in the corner, still shaking with fright. Sensitive animals, dogs.

\*     \*     \*

We would like to think of the following story about a naval rating as true, but our nasty cynical outlook prevents us from accepting even the best-authenticated stories without reservations, thus missing, as we are frequently told, a good deal of the fun in life. It appears that the young naval rating was gifted with pretty wizard eyesight and for this reason was picked for the stimulating, but slightly unenviable, job of standing on the bridge during enemy action and predicting the pattern of falling bombs from hostile aircraft—port or starboard, ahead or astern. On his reports the helmsman acted (he explained) with the utmost promptitude. One

day, standing on the bridge and watching a stick of bombs whizzing (according to his reckoning) comfortably to starboard he was seized by a sudden and uncontrollable urge to experiment. "Direct hit, Sir," he prophesied blithely. They put him in irons. "The trouble with the Navy," he confided to our correspondent, "is that they have no sense of humour."

\* \* \*

Feudalism dies hard. Evidence that it still smoulders, awaiting only a few fruity port-laden puffs from the old squire, is at hand. A friend who had been called up recently was discussing his prospects in the Army with the window-cleaner, whose views on the modern democratic army would have gladdened the heart of Colonel Bingham. "'Course it's orlright for what you might call the *elements*, Sir!" he said, "but I just 'ate to see your sort of young gentleman goin' into the army as a private. I only 'ope they don't put you in with a lot of Cockneys." Our friend, writing from a hut crammed with the elements, says that he's having a pretty good time. "Fortunately," he adds, "they're all Cockneys."

In very bitter weather not long ago, when coal and plumbers were equally at a premium, two middle-aged men were walking home through the streets of a garrison town. It was shortly after half-past ten. The darkness was absolute. Only passing snatches of talk and song gave a clue to a scene of emptying pubs, and streets that were filling with soldiery homeward bound. Full of warm thoughts of youth and other wars, the two were neither surprised nor

shocked when they stumbled over what proved to be a man on all fours on the pavement. "Come on," they cried, hoisting the muttering fellow to his feet, "you're not so bad, old chap. It's only the cold night air——" At this point the man regained the pavement, and they went for him again. "Oh God!" cried a passionate voice from the darkness at their feet, "will *nobody* let me turn off the water at the main?"

\* \* \*

When highbrows unbend, lowering themselves with the effortless grace of a steam excavator, to popular levels, they creak in every joint. We read, with some slight interest, the controversy between A. P. Herbert and the editor of a weekly review. The editor had the

last word; he implied that he w a s merely having a jest a t A.P.H.'s e x p e n s e. "Cannot h e take it?" asked the e d i t o r. And that, we cannot help thinking, is the most brilliant hybrid of pedantic English and colloquial American we are likely to read this season.

\* \* \*

An R.A.F. friend of ours, an incurable fisherman, who, faced with duty or rising trout, will reluctantly take the trout, had sneaked off from his post the other day to snatch an hour or two of peace with pipe and rod.

No sooner had he assembled the latter than a family party, picnic bent, arrived on the scene: Mother, Aunty, two nippers—a girl and a boy. At the same moment the sirens started. Gunfire followed the sirens closely.

Helped by Aunty, a brisk and practical woman, our R.A.F. friend packed the family into a dry ditch, at a point where the outgrowing trunk of a tree gave reasonable shelter—but let him tell it in his own words.

"Things happened quickly. The dive bombers were in Vic formation. As each peeled off in its dive and wailed down out of sight behind the hill that hid the town ('Cor! We got 'im!' said the little boy) the uproar broke out afresh. The big guns bayed, the little guns yelped and stuttered, and the blanketing thunder of heavy bombs intermittently blotted out other sounds. A cloud rose up from behind the hill. Hurricanes weaved in and out like sparrowhawks down a hedgerow. The smaller children were mildly scared: the older ones frankly interested. Shrapnel was falling everywhere.

"Nearby, some cows had

started to circle their field at a matronly canter. And then Mother became articulate. 'Look at them poor cows!' she wailed. 'Look at them—frightened out of their wits! It's a shame, that's what it is —it's a living shame!' "

*Lemuel Gulliver.*

## By Quentin Reynolds

# The Night of September 7th

SEPTEMBER used to be just another month. It was a nice enough month; cooler than August and not as cold as October. September used to mean that the cricket season was finished and that football had come into its own. It's different now. To those of us who have lived in London during the past year, September will always mean something else. September will forever mean the month THAT NASTY MAN started after us in real earnest. And September 7th will forever remain an important anniversary to us.

Most anniversaries are welcome —Christmas, New Year, St. George's Day, Whit Monday, the August Bank Holiday: these are joyous occasions. September 7th is a different kind of anniversary. On September 7th, 1940, more than four hundred men, women and children were killed in London by bombs. All of them were civilians. Late that night the German wireless boasted of the great performance by the Luftwaffe in bombing London.

As long as we live we should remember that boast. September 7th will remind us of it. It will remind us that the hatred we now feel for the German nation, for the German way of living, must be a permanent feeling for those of us who live under the democratic form of government and who think that life under any other form of government is intolerable. September 7th should remind us always of . . .

It was a bright afternoon and Kent, bathed by the sun, looked fresh and green. There was no warning. The pilots were sitting in their mess. Through the loudspeaker, came the curt command to take off. "Fifty plus heading this way," the C.O. of the station said. "Fifty plus" can mean anything. It might mean fifty airplanes or five hundred. It didn't matter to the pilots of this squadron. It was a good squadron. It had gotten thirty-seven German airplanes in one day over Dunkirk. Between May 14th and May 30th this squadron had downed sixty-five

German airplanes. These are official Air Ministry figures.

The squadron took off. Twelve fighter airplanes zoomed up to meet the "fifty plus." An hour and a half later an airplane wobbled to a landing on the aerodrome. The pilot climbed down wearily. He went into the mess. There wasn't much left of it. Some of the German bombs had found their marks. The telephone had gone. In fact, all communications had gone, and the C.O. had been ordered to transfer his headquarters to another aerodrome. The pilot sat down, wondering where his fellow pilots were. But none of them walked into the mess. Finally came the bitter realisation that he was the only survivor of that magnificent squadron.

The roar of a motor-cycle broke the silence of that bright September afternoon. An R.A.F. messenger walked in and asked for the C.O.

"I have an order from Fighter Command," he said. "The order is for your squadron to patrol at 16,000 feet over Dover."

He went out alone, climbed into his airplane, and took off. He patrolled at 16,000 feet over Dover. It was probably a bit difficult for him to keep his mind on flying. But orders were orders. The men of the R.A.F. don't ask questions. He patrolled at 16,000 feet. He flew into the sun, looking for German airplanes, looking for those who had killed his friends.

Every time September 7th comes around, I'll think of that boy up there alone, representing a squadron that didn't exist. I'll think of the neighbours of mine who died that day in London. It will remind me never to relax my hatred for Nazism, and the thraldom which Nazism would impose on the world.

### By Julian Huxley

# The Zoo's First Blitz

THE first bad blitz on the Zoo was on September 26th. It seems to be a general experience that having something to do in a raid seems much less alarming (even if actually more dangerous) than sitting in a shelter wondering how much closer the next bomb will be. That certainly was my own experience, as I helped to extinguish a fire or guided the A.F.S. men to the sea-lion pond to get a new supply of water (the main having been put out of action by a bomb).

But Zoos also provide their own special problems in air-raids. About one in the morning, by the light of the flames from a burning refreshment bar, a zebra was seen close to the offices. It turned out to be a stallion, liberated when an H.E. bomb had hit the Zebra House. He must later have found his way through the tunnel, for the next thing I heard was that he had escaped into the Outer Circle through the Timekeeper's Gate, and was making for Camden Town. A little generalship in deploying

reserves to cut off his retreat, and a good deal of mingled running and coaxing on the part of the main pursuing force, eventually got him back through the gate into the Stores Yard. There, however, he refused to enter the unfamiliar shed which had been opened for him. In fact, every attempt to drive him in, and every discharge of the neighbouring A.A. battery, caused him to back a little. The backing was in my direction, and I found myself wedged in a corner, with his hind hoofs not five feet away. I admit I was thankful when the animal suddenly changed his mind (as animals often do) and walked quietly into the shed.

Next morning I was telling his keeper about the incident, and confessing that I had been much more frightened by the proximity of the zebra's hoofs than by the possibility of bombs. "Why, you needn't have been frightened, sir," he replied; "he's a biter, not a kicker."

It was a pity I didn't know at the time which end I had something to fear from!

*"I couldn't find a four-inch, so I brought a couple of twos!"*

By Ritchie Calder

# September 7th in the Crypt

IT was what the Cockney with his gift for understatement called "a noisy night" last September. I was practising the gutter-flop in the back streets of Dockland. The clatter of the shrapnel was even more unnerving than the scream of the bombs. Incident had piled upon incident. Havoc had been let loose in East London. It was after midnight before I called in on my friend, Mickey the Midget. After hours of bombardment and barrage, of explosions and fires, I felt that even his shelter would be a refuge.

But Mickey, three feet six inches of confident nonchalance, was on his way to the Crypt. He was tinhatless, as he dodged with me across the road. We groped our way through the churchyard and pushed aside the damp, clammy draperies of the gas curtain, to be challenged by a sentinel shadow, who added to the impression that this was a kind of secret society. Mickey passed me through. We groped our way down into the murk of the Crypt. In these vaults were massive stone

sarcophagi. The heavy stone lids of these coffins had been levered off. The bones and dust of the centuries had been tipped out. The last resting-place of the dead had been claimed by the living and in one of them, as though he were lying in state, was a navvy, snoring blissfully and stirring up the bone dust with every snore. In a recess, by the light of trembling candleflames, a macabre card school was playing solo. Their card-table was a tomb. The new death was so near that the old dead had no reality.

We picked our way through huddles of old men and women, cramped on narrow benches or sprawled in the narrow aisles. It was bitterly cold and with every bomb thud, the sandwich board, "Sinners Repent or Ye Perish,"

which had been used to block a window, flapped, a grim reminder that the half-submerged window was blacked-out, not blocked-up.

Mickey the Midget scrambled ahead of me up a hen-ladder to the family pews recessed in the wall and as I peered over the ledge, I was confronted by a brown baby face with startled black eyes under a turban. The black eyes goggled in the flickering candle light and then the baby disappeared under the bedclothes beside its Indian mother. Stretched majestically on the rough floor was the long figure of an ex-Bengal lancer with his shovel beard spread over the

blanket, his head turbanned. A cockney family was asleep in a niche above.

The squalor of this crypt, like most of the shelters last September, was indescribable. It seemed then as though humanity had descended into a pit of degradation, out of which it could never struggle. . . .

Mickey the Midget took me back in 1941. The candles had given place to electric light. The tomb-card-table had given place to a buffet. Filthy bedclothes to tidy bunks. And, solemn monument to London's sanity, porcelain water closets had swept away the sarcophagi.

*" This one doesn't talk much — but he's a great reader"*

*Saint Paul's of London*
1. *St. Paul's Cathedral has always been the pride of London. During the blitz
it became something more – a symbol of defiance and endurance, something almost personal.
This picture shows the aftermath of an air raid – in the foreground a mass of stinking
rags, beyond it St. Paul's, with its eastern windows blown in, but still serene and dominant.*

*2. Seen from across the river, from Southwark Street, through the windows of a blitzed warehouse. The humble houses in the foreground, with their boarded-up windows and the black chimneys of the power house behind them, are essentially parts of that body of which the Cathedral dome is, as it were, the head.*

*3. From Bankside; 'Under the cross of gold That shines over city and river,'
wrote Tennyson. Here it is shining over sombre warehouses, sailing-barges whose cargo
is rubbish and refuse, and a pair of swans that might have sailed into this picture out of
the poem by Spenser. But in Spenser's day the Cathedral was Gothic.*

4. *Seen from the Temple St. Paul's stands head-on with its two clock towers as level and placid as fire-dogs. Its unscathed dome consoles us for the desolation in the foreground. On the left against the sky is Wren's tallest spire, which stands over a church that is now a shell. 'Got no insides,' Say the bells of St. Bride's.*

5. *A picture taken from the tower of St. Mary-le-Bow, another victim of the raids. Through the iron scaffolding we look down on a valley of dry bones. A sea of destruction seems to have flowed right up to the Cathedral — and then turned back, having merely splashed its walls. (Notice the pockmarks from bomb-splinters.)*

*Back stage at the Windmill: ten minutes to the show*
*Once inside a theatre, you breathe electric air. The lights are brighter, the*
*shadows darker, than in the world outside. A lost hairpin becomes a tragedy.*
*A passing joke becomes high comedy. A second of time becomes important as an hour.*
*Brandt catches all this eager tension in these photographs of back-stage scenes.*

**By Lesley Osmond**

# September at the Windmill

I CAN still see Sonia wearing a couple of roses, a tin helmet, and her first-aid bag!

The Stage Manager had called to us on the microphone: "Our roof-spotters tell us there are enemy 'planes overhead. The curtain has been lowered. All first-aid girls take up their positions."

That was on September 7th.

I remember going along with the five other girls to fetch our kit. Sonia, who was one of them, took up her position in the lounge where the audience had gathered round the bar. I am not surprised that they were disappointed when the show started again; anyone would feel safe with Sonia around!

That night most of us slept in the theatre. Next morning the cleaners put on the lights to tidy up in the stalls. They were very surprised when two tousled heads appeared over the edge of the stage box, yelling "Put out those lights."

After that Saturday we never stopped the show again. We settled down to live in the theatre. Although we often went out for supper, it was a wonderful feeling coming back, shutting the stage door and hurrying downstairs to join the others tucked up on their mattresses in the dressing-rooms.

One night Charmian came in, a little muddy and untidy.

"I was forced to fall flat on my face with a completely strange sailor outside Lyons Corner House!" she told me with dignity.

When we were making our beds on the floor one night we heard a bomb whistle over our heads. Instinctively everyone fell on their faces, except one girl who jumped on a chair and screamed.

Then we all jumped up and screamed. A small paper bag was slowly moving across the floor!

There was a mouse inside it!

"What," we said, "is a bomb *outside* compared with a mouse *inside*?"

Looking back on those days, I seem to remember the times when we laughed and forget the times when we were frightened.

Thanks to my grand blitz companions! As we often say, "What is a blitz amongst friends!"

# Eros

### By Olga Katzin

*Eros is vanished from Piccadilly,*
*Who loosed his shafts at the circling cars,*
*Silver-winged in the daybreak chilly,*
*Swift and flying under the stars.*
*Generals pacing along Whitehall*
*Must keep their watch though the heavens fall,*
*And ride the raids out, willy nilly,*
*But the love-god flees from the face of Mars.*

*News of battle has sent him packing,*
*From his island perch he has fluttered down,*
*His radiant godhead wrapped in sacking*
*Gay and naked from sole to crown.*
*Stout stone worthies still throng the city,*
*Whose loss or absence none would pity*
*But the heartbeat of London's life is lacking-*
*Eros is driven away from town.*

*London's lovers are left benighted,*
*Winter sunshine more palely glows,*
*The site is sealed where his foot alighted,*
*The young, the laughing, the lost Eros.*
*Fled is the gleam of his pagan graces*
*From the sandbagged streets and the anxious faces,*
*A guardian presence no longer sighted*
*The heart of poetry in London's prose.*

*We'll not believe that the war is ended*
*When peace is signed with a golden pen,*
*Or doom averted that long impended*

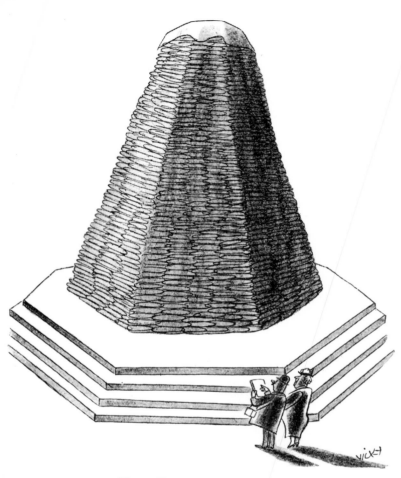

*"It says 'Eros' – Epstein, I presume"*

For streets and rooftrees and gods and men,
But when he alights in the midnight stilly
To bend his bow over Piccadilly,
From his bonds set free, from the sky descended,
We'll know that the war is over then.

**18 miles**

**1 ½ pints**

**170 million candles**

# Life in the Army

**11 buttons**

**38 ounces**

| | | |
|---|---|---|
| Day's march | .. | 18 miles |
| Major General's pay | £1,652 p.a. | |
| Weight of tin helmet | 38 ounces. | |
| Hours of work (recruit) | | 34 per week. |
| Paces per minute | 70 slow march | |
| Searchlight's power | | 170 million candle power |
| Buttons on coat (infantryman) | 11 | |
| Eyesight minimum requirements for infantrymen | | 4/10 in. letters at 20 ft. |
| Minimum height (recruit) | | 5 ft. 2 in. |
| Men in a platoon .. | .. | 39 |
| Weight of shell (large) | 1,938 lb. | |
| Water bottle capacity | 1½ pints | |
| Weight of rifle | .. | 8 lb. 10 oz. |
| Cost of uniform (officers) .. | £40 | |
| Morse buzzer signaller | | 10 words a minute |
| Length bayonet blade | .. | 22 in. |

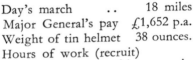

**34 hours' work**

**5 ft. 2 in.**

**£1,652**

**1,938 lb.**

**Eyesight minimum**

# THE FIRST WEEK

## Out of the Diary of a Recruit

*ILLUSTRATIONS BY JAMES BOSWELL*

**MONDAY.** Letters come at 4 p.m. We cluster round the Orderly Corporal, hoping against reason, like sparrows about a dead horse. There can't possibly be anything for us. We only got here this morning. We put on Battle Dress at 1.30, and have got our first military flavour. It's only a flavour as yet. We are no more like soldiers than a fishy fork is like fish. Bits of our first Army hair-cut cling to our ears. A Corporal looks in at us and says, "Why should England tremble? My God." We are in our Hut: thirty beds made of three boards and two trestles; a stove; some brooms and a shovel. We have been told to make ourselves at home. One man has already filled half of a fourpenny pad with his new sorrows, and, concluding with, "But

don't worry, Dear Mum, I am quite all right," asks for a stamp. Nobody talks. It is raining. There is nothing round here but mud and grass. The grass is dead. No doubt it is better off. Somebody keeps asking: "But *do* they put Something in the Tea?" A Sergeant says: "Anybody here like potatoes?" Four of us pluck up courage to say "Yes." "Then come and peel some," says the Sergeant. He adds: "All joking aside, I'm looking for somebody who can sing or play the piano." Three more leap up eagerly. One says he can play an accordeon. "You'll do," says the Sergeant,

"Come and help with the dustbins." The day ends. Lights go out. A man from Worksop screams in his sleep. Another, from Kent, stops breathing with a sharp *Khuk*, and then struggles desperately, finally getting his breath back with a *Wahooooo!*

**TUESDAY.** An Officer informs us of Army Law. Everything is illegal, particularly Mutiny, Drunkenness, Insubordination, Gambling, Filthy Talk, Unclean Habits and Boots, Desertion, Neglect of Duty, Answering Back, Dumb Insolence, Stealing, Looting, Failure To Respect Woman-hood, Murder, Cowardice, Swapping Kit, Bribery, Idleness, Possessing Playing Cards, Bringing Alcohol Into Barracks, Masquerading As An Officer Or N.C.O., Fighting Whilst On Active Service, and Urinating Outside The Hut But Not In The Proper Place. The only indoor game officially permitted is Lotto, or Housie-Housie. If we want to go and drink, we must do so in the proper place: in Barracks, the Naffy. If we want to go and desert, we must be prepared to face the consequences. These consequences make Parkhurst seem like the wide open spaces. The Sergeant asks if we are getting used to it. We enthusiastically cry, "Oh

yes." To-morrow we shall be given our first taste of the Square. In the meantime, to occupy our minds, there is some swabbing to do. We swab. We receive a Stab In The Arm to inoculate us against diseases. We have one Anti-Vaccinist who swears he will die a thousand deaths rather than submit. But when he opens his mouth to protest, words will not come. He is stabbed. We go to the Naffy. Compared with the pies, the tea seems good. *Night:* The man from Worksop dreams

he is saving my life in deep water.

**WEDNESDAY.** The Square. The Sergeant says: "What a shower of tripe you are! What horrible men! Gimme loaves to turn into fishes. Gimme water to turn into wine. But turn you into Soldiers, . . .! Groo! Why do some mothers have sons?" We leave the Square, sore of foot and heart, for Weapon Training. Then, P.T. The Staff Sergeant looks at us and we sweat in anticipation. Rumour has it that he once put his fist through a galvanised iron wash-bowl. He makes us run round and round, and jump up and down, and fall flat, and skip-jump, and carry each other in our arms, and crouch, and stretch, and breathe in and out, and hop, and hang on bars, and roll over on mats, and vault over horses. Wednesday is a short day, a half-holiday. The man with the fourpenny pad fills a foolscap envelope with a catalogue of atrocious sufferings, but, concluding asks how you spell "Enjoyable." We are led out in due course for a Medical. We have to appear, nakedly, before the M.O. I do not know what he is looking for: he doesn't seem to find it. He looks bored. Somebody asks what these examinations are for. A theorist suggests that once upon a time a lady called Sweet Polly Oliver joined the Army, and since then they cannot be too careful. It seems that there is a little town in reach of an infrequent bus, and that in this little town there are Goings On. Our informant makes it sound like Hollywood in the 1920's. Research lays bare the fact that in the little town nothing whatever goes on. There is a tea-shop which is usually shut, and a cinema to which *Broadway Melody* has just come. The girls, it appears, are

all engaged to N.C.O.'s. Such as are not know soldiers only too well. *Night:* The man from Worksop dreams of a Charlie Chaplin film he once saw.

**THURSDAY.** P.T. Square. Weapon Training. Square. Shepherd's Pie for Dinner. Lecture on Hygiene: contagious diseases are catching, and also illegal. More Square. Gas Masks fitted in gas-chamber. Tear-gas makes our eyes water. We pretend to weep, saying "Boo-Hoo." Tea. Hut. Bed. Man from Worksop talks in sleep of Uncle's Tumour in Throat, "Big as a Babby's Head." Stiff all over.

**FRIDAY.** As we rise, we cry "Eek." Our muscles are knotted. Man from Kent claims that, such is the rush in the wash-house, he cleaned man from Worksop's teeth. P.T., "to loosen us up";

then Square, to tighten us up; then more of the same. *Afternoon:* some fatigues, concerned with dead leaves. We are acquiring a technique of keeping a lookout while relaxing. *Evening:* The Man with the Four-penny Pad has come down to seven lines. We had biscuits for tea: he enclosed one in envelope, saying, "This is the kind of thing we get. But don't worry. I am quite at home."

**SATUR-DAY.** Half-day. Most of us sleep. Others, fearing fatigues, hide about Camp. I

don't know what's happened: I have been asleep. P.T., and Drill have got me in the legs. I do not believe I have much longer to live. Worksop has been talking for three hours about how they had to give him salt-water after his wedding-breakfast. The rain is heavier. The mud is deeper. It is amazing how soft the beds are now. Perhaps this is because deal is a nice soft wood. Or it may be the air. One sleeps.

**SUNDAY.** Sunday like any other Sunday, except that there is Church. Day of rest, apart from scrubbing out hut, beds, utensils, windows, stove, coal-tub, buckets, and anything else that is wash-able. An examination of the Library reveals *Little Arthur's England, Angela's First Term,* the *Complete Works of Mrs. Humphrey Ward, Trixie's Fairy, The Pilgrim's Progress,* 198 pages of a *Life of Nelson,* and a bound vol-ume of *House-hold Words.* We talk of wine, Relativity, wo-men, Hitler, song, Ann Sheridan, chil-dren, bicycles, mothers, beetroots, gangsters, tumours, sergeants, ghosts, Godfrey Winn, the poten-tialities of nurses, dum-dum bullets, the weather, toffee-apples, and the War. Soon we shall go to bed. Then Lights Out will sound. Then the man from Worksop will start to talk of his friend's grandmother who married again at eighty-nine. Then we shall sleep, accepting, with incredulous astonishment, the certainty that tomorrow will be Monday and we've been here a whole week.

**By Adolf Hitler**

# My New Year Resolutions

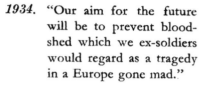

*The following are promises made by Hitler in his New Year speeches since 1934.*

*1934.* "Our aim for the future will be to prevent bloodshed which we ex-soldiers would regard as a tragedy in a Europe gone mad."

*1935.* "Without Peace prosperous progress is not to be hoped for in any human activity."

*1936.* "Our chief goal will be to preserve external Peace."

*1937.* "No conflict is possible between France and Germany."

*1938.* "The rebirth of the German people will not be achieved by making onslaughts abroad."

*1939.* "The Establishment of our new Unity has made possible the solution of the great European question (of German Lebensraum) without a War."

*1940.* "For long centuries Germany and Russia lived side by side in Peace. Why not in future too? Each attempt to make it impossible will be frustrated because the motives of such attempts will be clearly understood by all."

*1941.* "The year 1941 will see the completion of victory . . . the greatest in our history."

*"Of course, you realise, Mervyn, I can't do this every time"*

## By T. Thompson

# Just Like a Mother

"NOW if yo have any grievances," said the Corporal, "just trot 'em out to me. Ah'm just like a mother to my lads."

"Well," said the Recruit, "wheer's th' tablecloth?"

"Tablecloth!" said the Corporal in amazement. "Did Ah hear thee say tablecloth?"

"Me mother allus lays a tablecloth," said the Recruit.

"Tha should ha' brought thi mother wi' thee," said the Corporal. "Tha'rt in th' army . . . not at th' Ritz."

"Sergeants has a tablecloth," said the Recruit. "Ah've seen 'em."

"Ah know Sergeants has a tablecloth," said the Corporal. "Tha has to work thi way up to a tablecloth."

"Ah don't see why there shouldn't be a tablecloth," said the Recruit. "We're all 'uman bein's."

"Ah wouldn't say that," said the Corporal. "Not in th' Army. Anyway, not under two stripes."

"If Ah ever meet th' gaffer Ah'll tell him," said the Recruit.

"Th' gaffer?" said the Corporal.

"Aye," said the Recruit. "Th' gaffer. Th' boss."

"Ah see," said the Corporal. "Who did tha meet when tha jined?"

"He wor in blue," said the Recruit. "An' he swore somefink awful."

"Th' Padre," said the Corporal. "Tha should ha' seen th' Brigadier. Never bother wi' th' understrappers."

"Never seen sich a 'ole as this," said the Recruit. " Miles to walk for a packet of fags."

"Save yer money," said the Corporal.

"Money!" said the Recruit. "Ah never got none yet. When do they pay an' how often?"

"There's been some misunderstandin' 'ere," said the Corporal. "Did they not give thee a cheque book when tha jined?"

"Ah never got nowt," said the Recruit. "Nobbut a dirty look."

"Thee leave it to me," said the

Corporal. "Ah'll reduce some-body for this."

"They tell me they put in a lot o' o'ertime on this station," said the Recruit. "Do they pay time-an'-a-half for o'ertime?"

"Well, well," said the Corporal. "That's an idea. Ah don't think th' question's ever arose afore. Ah'll put it to 'em if tha likes."

"Put it to who?" said the Recruit.

"Na then," said the Corporal. "Tha's put thi finger on th' weak spot. These Cabinet Ministers are in an' out like wind in a bottle. If a question like that geet to th' wrong chap it might mean a secret session."

"Ah don't want to cause no trouble," said the Recruit.

"That's the true army sperrit," said the Corporal. "It'll all be on thi bounty."

"Me bounty?" said the Recruit.

"Aye," said the Corporal. "If tha survives ... tha gets a bounty."

"What if Ah don't survive?" said the Recruit.

"Ah'll speak for thee a table-cloth," said the Corporal, "Ah'm as good as a mother to my lads."

## by J. Maclaren-Ross

# I've Been Locked Up Before

IN the guardroom at the depot, where the Inlying Picket used to sleep, they had those double-decker beds in rows, and the springs of the beds were always getting broken. One night they had all new beds in, and the next night they were all broken again.

Of course, on Inlying Picket you had to sleep with all your equipment on, and no doubt that helped to break the springs; anyway, they hung down like nets and your equipment'd get inextricably caught up in them.

Naturally, as soon as you came off parade outside there was a dash for the guardroom, and the thing to do was to get a bed that wasn't broken, or at any rate less broken than the rest, and to avoid the beds that were sandwiched in the middle, because if you had one of those you were hopelessly bottled up when it came to your turn for going out on guard, or if the alarm went.

I remember one night I got in there last and all the beds had been bagged except a top one that had no springs in it at all. It looked as though I'd have to stand up all night, but then one of the military police came and said did I mind sleeping in a cell, and I said No, so he took me in there and said did I mind being locked in because of rules and regulations and also there was a prisoner in the next cell, the one who'd shot his thumb off and they weren't certain how: he'd been in the clink a month

now awaiting court-martial.

Anyway, this M.P. locked me in and I went to sleep; they'd a smashing bed in there. I was due to go on picket outside at four in the morning, and the sergeant banged on the door then and said, Wakey, wakey, rise and shine. I said, Let me out, I'm locked in, and the M.P. came and said, You've got the key. I said, No, you've got it, and he said, I gave it to you. Neither of us could find it though, and we all shouted and hammered and said we hadn't got the key, and the prisoner hammered on the wall of his cell and said, Here, I want some mucking sleep—is it the invasion or what?

Eventually the key was found on the floor of the guardroom and everything was all right. Another man did my picket because I couldn't get out in time. Lucky the alarm didn't go though, because I'd the Bren gun and the anti-tank rifle in there with me and most of the ammunition boxes that hadn't been used to prop up beds with as well.

However, that's another story, the night I got locked in the cell. This is one about Gas. I've got them mixed, it was a different night.

We'd each chosen a bed and were laying out our bedding when suddenly the runner came dashing in. He was a Category C man, a Cockney with all sorts of things wrong with him, and many of them wrong with his face. He'd a most extraordinary face, but you couldn't see it now because he'd his respirator on over it and through the respirator he yelled out, GAS!

We said, Cut it out, and the sergeant said, Pack it in, I've a mind to shove you on report play-arsing about a thing like that. But the runner said, Honest, sarge, it IS gas, no kidding. He was in a proper stew.

So the sergeant went out and the corporal, too, and they came back with their eyes streaming and shouted, He's right, lads, get 'em on. We out with our respirators and had them adjusted quicker than we'd ever done it on gas drill, and there was hell being kicked up. Then the sergeant shouted, Ssh, and we listened and we could hear Jerry going over, and the sergeant said, He must just have dropped it, and the runner said, See, I was right.

WELL, we were all of a doodah, not frightened, we were too excited for that I think, but all rushing to and fro, and some of us went out and, yes, it was gas right enough, but what kind? How should I know, the sergeant said, I've never been on a gas course, get the gas sergeant. The runner went off. Meantime I got out my notebook with all about gas in it and which smelt of rotten fruit and which of musty hay, and they all crowded round trying to read it through their respirators.

Anyway, we said, it isn't DICK because that has no smell and this had; it was tear gas because you could feel it pricking your throat where you'd shaved, and the runner came back and said the gas sergeant had gone on the

beer downtown, but that round the stores the gas was much worse and the gas sentry raising Cain. So the 'phone orderly rang up for the gas officer; nobody could remember which one it was though, because they'd changed them and one had been posted, but which?

Meantime the sergeant said, Come on, and five of us went with him up the Lines by the Company store, and you could feel the gas there, like when you went through the chamber.

There was a light on in the store, you could see it under the door. The sergeant shouted OPEN UP, and there was the storeman staggering about with his eyes running and no respirator on and the gas came from in there—it was terrific.

Anyway, it turned out he'd knocked over a crate of tear gas bombs, and some had gone off, and the storeman said, Why all this fuss, he'd got the worst of it anyway 'cause his respirator had been knocked off by some swine in the Naffy night before. The sergeant said, Serve you right putting the wind up us that way, and then they argued and the sergeant said, Shut up.

By this time the gas officer had arrived, the one that hadn't been posted, and he heard the story and there was trouble. But in the end they decided not to make a Thing about it, and the sergeant said should he include it in his guard report, and it was decided No.

So maybe I shouldn't be writing about it now, as maybe it's SECRET and they might have me on a court-martial. But hell, why worry: it wouldn't be the first time I've been locked in a cell.

"At the command 'Escort and accused shun! Quick march! Brace up!
Left, right, left, right! Put bags of pride and swank into it!!! . . .'"

*"Wot cheer, Nelson!"*

by Alan Jenkins

# "On the Hands—Down!"

THE recruits trot in, shivering, their greatcoats over their little vests and shorts, like outsize bath-robes. Regretfully they shed their coats in the changing-room. A few, vaccinated only yesterday, are in some pain. White-skinned, thin, malnourished, city-bred, they stand uncertainly along the wall to hear the Sergeant-Major's introductory speech. He regards them with misgivings:

"You know why you're here, don't you? There's a job to be done. We've got to turn you into hard men, God help you. We need gunners with brains workin' quick as what their 'ands and feet do. The Hun's got seven years' start on us in this fitness game. You'll get to enjoy it. You'll be a pack of damn fools if you don't take advantage of what we teach you. Instructors—call the roll!"

Bombardier B. Wetherby takes charge.

Some of the recruits remember him as Freddy Schwarz, the lightweight in Civvy Street. Like most Army P.T. men, he has cultivated a musical intonation, a high elocuting voice, a touch of the theatre, now snapping, now gay, now brutal, sometimes almost feminine. He sneers, cajoles, pleads, commands; but never stops talking.

"Running in a circle round me —*be*-gin. Raise those knees, *raise* 'em. On your toes—there, that's pretty. On all fours — *down*. 'Strewth, I never saw such a lot of old women, anyone'd think you was three months gorn. Left turn, right turn, about turn, sit down, stand up! Left leg—*raise:* right leg—*raise:* both legs—*raise* . . . Eh, that shook yer, didn't it?

"Pay attention, you. What was you in civvy life, a blinkin' West End sissy? Don't look at me like that, mate—I ain't got B.O. Touch the four walls of the Gym—*go!* Four teams facing me—*go!*"

He turns round and round, roaring with mirth, the teams vainly trying to face him.

"All right, lads, I won't kill you, not to-day any road. Class— rest. Astride for deep breathing —jump. Legs *wide* apart, Gawd strewth, you needn't be afraid anything'll drop out! Shoulder-rolling—*be*-gin. Faster, faster—look at me, *I* can do it, for all I was with my young lady last night. Coo, I never. saw such a lot o' constipated nuns!

"When I tell you *and not before*, every man chase the bloke next to him and try to pull down his trousers — *go!*" Bombardier Wetherby greets this performance with an unprintable witticism.

"Class, atten-*shon*. Sit down. Take your shoes off. Barefoot running—begin. Cures 'ammer toes, so they tell me. Shoes *on*: Run three times round yer thumb—*go!* Fall out all men over sixty-five. What, none of yer? You look like you was linin' up for yer old age pensions. 'Ow old are you, Darkie? Nineteen? Cor, you should have bags of life in you. Nineteen! You're young, you're full of go, and you 'olds yerself like the 'Unchback of Notre-Damn-All. . . .

"Right, we'll have a game. When I say Do This, you Do It. When I say Do That, you Don't. Get it? Anyone I catch out goes down on the floor and does four arms-bends. . . . Take that grin orf your face. Stand *still*. Stand on your hands—*naow*, I don't want no acrobatics, you just bends down and sticks yer 'ands under yer shoes, and I comes along and kicks yer behind in this manner, so . . . eh, you're half a-bloody-sleep, all of you. Watcher think you are—the Russian Ballitt?"

Puny bodies writhe and groan. One owlish little man's spectacles are steamed over with sweat. Skinny arms and legs quiver, strive, crumple exhausted. ·

"And just *one* more . . ." beseeches Bombardier Wetherby tragically. "Another one for *me*. And one for the Colonel. And one for Max Miller. And one for the Royal Family—lucky people!"

He fills in the time with a dozen or so neat handsprings. Critically he examines the collapsed bodies, tousling their heads affectionately, calling them Lofty and Tich and Oscar and Sessil and Ginger and Blondy.

"Coo, you don't wanter be scared of exercise," he chuckles as he dismisses the class. "The Army takes full responsibility if you break yer blinkin' necks!"

# FRUSTRATION

**By John Pudney**

# Food Rationing

## Lack of Restraint

*I find it puts me out of humour*
*To be described as "the consumer."*
*More accurate, more British, neater,*
*I would I were described "the eater."*

## Debauchee

*A certain type*
*Eats tripe,*
*While others*
*Eat their wives' mothers.*
*Only an utter*
*Debauchee regards butter*
*As an essential addition*
*To either nutrition.*

## Then I Says to Her . . .

*Think of the host*
*Who chatted over buttered toast.*
*And will they talk so large*
*On toast and marge?*

## Col. Tonnage Hurt

*"It's hard upon the better sort*
*Of person," Col. Tonnage snorted*
*"It takes one's mind off stocks and*
*    sport*
*To have one's breakfast thwarted."*

## War-Time Anthem For the Stout

*Ounces, I fear*
*Are here.*
*So we can fling away stones*
*Bless our bones!*
*And treat flesh*
*Afresh.*

## Civilisations Are Never the Same

*In Babylon*
*They would carry on*
*With short rations without slanging,*
*So long as their gardens kept hanging.*
*But in Ealing,*
*The lack of higher feeling*
*Causes quite recumbent gardens to be*
*    shaken*
*By a mere rationing of bacon.*

## You Should Have Heard . . .

*My tale of Florrie Urk is sad.*
*She took the ration books from Dad;*
*And spread the coupons on her bread.*
*"A wartime substitute," she said.*

"'With a half-human howl the Hooded Terror disappeared into the gathering gloom . . .' O.K. Corp., off with the lights and let's get some sleep"

by Lionel Davidson

# Goodnight, Deanna

O N the seamen's mess-deck the hands were turned in, when A.B. Hicks, speaking into the darkness from his hammock, said: "What was that picture with Deanna Durbin and Charles Laughton?"

The three other hands who were awake said "Eh?" together, so that within a few seconds twenty heads were up inquiring what was the buzz.

"That picture with Deanna Durbin and Charles Laughton," said A.B. Hicks. "What was the name of it?"

"I believe it was called 'It Started with Eve,'" said the O.D. politely. (He was the only Ordinary Seaman present and his position was lowly.)

"You mean where she sang *Ave Maria?*" said A.B. Maxwell.

"That was in 'A Hundred Men and a Girl,'" said the O.D.

Stripy, the Leading Hand of the Mess, shifted his bulk in his hammock. "If that's the O.D. cackling, e'd better get 'is 'ead down," he said.

There was silence for a few moments, then A.B. Hicks said: "I remember it well, but I just can't think of the name."

"Ah," said A.B. Maxwell. "It'll be where she sings *Ave Maria.* 'San Francisco,' it was called."

"San Francisco me Aunt Fanny," said A.B. Smigget. "Alice Faye was in that. I saw it in Reykjavik, Iceland."

"Course I wasn't with the 'Ome Fleet myself," retorted A.B. Maxwell, with biting sarcasm, "but I remember the picture well. Saw it at the Cape last year. Deanna Durbin it was."

"When was you at the Cape?" said A.B. Smigget.

"January last year, in the old *Stoat.*"

"Ho, the *Stoat,* eh? When was that floating gash-bin ever at the Cape?"

A.B. Maxwell's head shot up.

"When was we at the Cape? Only since the Madagascar pass-up, that's all. Bit before your time, but we left the Eastern Fleet in September and worked the Cape for seven months."

A.B. Hawkes, dozing off, broke into the conversation.

"Eastern Fleet in September? Bit adrift there, ain't you? I was there last September, with the *Prosperous,* and there was no *Stoat* then."

"Ha!" said A.B. Smigget.

"Not last September, goon," cried Maxwell. "Oo said last September? The one before."

"Just can't think of it," said A.B. Hicks. "I remember old Charles jitterbugs all over the place in it."

"I think I've got it in my kit-bag," said the O.D. "In a monthly cinema programme, but I'm almost sure it was called 'It Started with Eve.'"

Stripy awoke suddenly.

"Is that O.D. still cackling there?" he said. "You'll be liftin' yer lid on the

129

Quarter Deck to-morrow if you don't get turned in there, me lad."

"Ah, 'op out an' get it, there's a good bloke," said A.B. Hicks. "Can't sleep till I get that off me mind."

The O.D. swung himself out of his warm hammock, and started to search for his bag, which lay at the base of a great heap of thirty exactly similar bags.

"YES, I remember the picture you mean," said A.B. Hawkes, turning comfortably in his hammock. "It all takes place in Havana, and old what's-name—old Fred Astaire dances in it. There's old Exavier Cugat an' 'is band, too. Saw 'im when we was working from Kingston, Jamaica."

"Kingston, Jamaica," said A.B. Maxwell, "when was you at Kingston, Jamaica?"

"When was I at Kingston, Jamaica?" repeated A.B. Hawkes. "While you was doing boy's time, I expect, mate. After the *Graf Spee* pass-up, we was working Kingston, Jamaica, beginning of the war, in the old *Savage*."

"Ho, the *Savage*, eh?" said A.B. Maxwell with rich amusement. "I seem to remember a certain tub *Savage* ramming the *Thrush* in no seaway. Good visibility, I believe it was. I seem to remember the ship's company of this *Savage* dursn't go ashore for fear of getting thumped by the *Thrush*."

"Course, if anyone'd like to try an' thump me," began A.B. Hawkes, warmly, when A.B. Hicks said: "No, old Fred Astaire ain't in this one. In this picture, old Charles Laughton 'e's a millionaire, and Robert Cummings is 'is son that meets up with this party Deanna Durbin working in a shop.

She sells dresses."

"I 'ad a party in a dress shop," said A.B. Smigget quickly. "In Reykjavik, Iceland, it was. I went in this shop to get silk stockings for the party at 'ome, and not knowing the size she 'ad to guess it by 'er own leg."

"Go on," said the O.D. suddenly, with appreciation. "What happened?"

Stripy sat up in his hammock.

"I've warned you, my lad," he said. "If I 'ave to 'op out there to you, you'll know about it. Now get turned in there, and that's the last time."

A.B. Hicks, looking over the side of his hammock, saw that the O.D. had managed to find his bag and was now struggling to extricate it.

"Ah, got it, 'ave yer," he said. "Good lad. Chop chop and get that programme out then."

"This party in Reykjavik, Iceland," said A.B. Smigget.

"'Orrible 'abit they've got in Iceland of chargin' you up for silk stockings," said A.B. Maxwell. "Now at the Cape 'and Durban they throw 'em at you. Jack's the boy out there."

"This party in Reykjavik, Iceland," said A.B. Smigget.

"I think I've almost got the name of it," said A.B. Hicks, suddenly. "On the tip of my tongue it is."

"I saw it up in Reykjavik, Iceland," said A.B. Smigget desperately. "She sings 'Waltzin' in the Clouds' in it."

"That was 'Spring Parade,'" said the O.D. involuntarily.

Stripy awoke with a fearsome snuffle.

"You can't say I 'aven't warned you," he said grimly. "Now stand by for fourpennorth."

"The lad's talkin' in 'is sleep," said

A.B. Hicks quickly, peering over the side of his hammock, and observing that the O.D. had managed to extricate his bag and had dragged it to the bulkhead emergency lamp.

"Well, thump 'is ear," said Stripy. "O.D.'s nattering all night, keepin' the mess awake! Thump 'im quick or 'e'll 'ave to sleep on deck."

Waiting only for the few seconds to elapse before the bulkheads reverberated to the rich, full-toned snore that testified the Leading Hand was deep again in his slumbers, Hicks spoke urgently to the O.D.

"You'll 'ave us all in the rattle if you don't look sharp," he said, sternly. "Chop chop there, my son."

At half-past three in the morning, the O.D., his neck aching in a draught of air from the ventilator shaft, eyes pricking with lack of sleep, had turned out his bag. At the bottom, in the pocket of a neatly-folded jumper, he discovered with weary satisfaction the cinema programme. He brought it near to the dim lamp, and saw the announcement " 'It Started With Eve,' Starring Deanna Durbin and Charles Laughton." He stretched stiffly up, and swung himself into his hammock with the programme.

In the next hammock, A.B. Hicks was soundly sleeping, a smile on his face. The O.D. gently shook him.

"I was right," he said, as the seaman blinked up at him, " 'It Started with Eve.' " A few billets along, Stripy stirred in his sleep.

"Did it, mate?" A.B. Hicks muttered throatily. "If that solid 'ead of your'n ain't down in ten seconds it'll end in a thump."

After a few moments of bitter meditation, the O.D. folded the programme, placed it carefully down the side of his hammock, and got his head down.

# How a Soldier Spends his Time

33·3% sleeping.
20% polishing, cleaning, blancoing kit.
16·6% drilling ⎫
16·6% thinking ⎬ (*simultaneous*).
about girls ⎭
Only 2% going out with girls (*more if Canadian, Polish, etc.*).
8·2% queueing.
4·15% eating.
4·5% drinking beer ⎫ (*simultaneous*).
4·5% grumbling ⎬
1·2% writing letters (1 *per week on Sunday*).
0·003% reading (*i.e., looking at pictures*).
0·0014% shaving.
0·00005% fighting.

*In the remaining* 0·05%

## HE SOMEHOW—

sews on 300 buttons a year,
using 166 yards of thread;
swears 144 times a day,
is sworn at 288 times a day;
stamps feet 200 times a day,
wearing out 4·7 ins. of leather
in a year;
laughs 58 times a day; and
salutes 84 times a day.

*"Do I need a caption?"*

GLASS

LON

*Sniper*

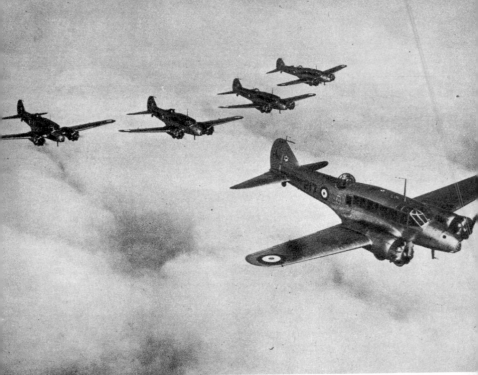

CENTRAL PRESS                                                                                 LON

*Reconnaissance*

KEYSTONE

LON

*Tank trap*

LE QUAY AUSTR

*"I'll see you next July"*

By Lionel Birch

# Leave, 1940

DOWN there, inside the chalk-covered trenches at Dover, last September, we used regularly to order up the most exotic food, the most exquisite wines.

Every day, as soon as the Cap Grisnez guns, or the dive-bombers over the harbour, sent us scurrying to our slit trenches, we un-typical recruits would summon the head-waiter of the Café Royal or the Czarda or Simpson's or Prunier's, or beckon to the patronne of that little place in Dean Street.

Pâté maison or oysters, bouilla-baisse or pipérade, roast grouse or jugged hare, zabaglione, camembert, green figs. The whole thing to be washed down with, successively, very dry Amontillado, Lieb-fraumilch, Château Mangaux, Courvoisier. The evening to be rounded off with a visit to the Nest, or the Nut-house, or the Paradise, or the Hungaria, with Vicky or Nina or Eve or Joan.

Oh! the greed—auntie dear!—and the materialism of us once-so-spoiled ex-civilian soldiers, plan-ning dinners and evenings down there in the slit trenches, while bombs whistled down on the har-bour—a safe half-mile away.

You may take a poor view of our taste; but those, undoubtedly, were the sort of things that we were going to eat and do, so soon as ever our forty-eight hours' leave should come round.

It was only when we did, at last, get our forty-eight, that we realised the revolutionary truth: there is no such thing as leave. Not in the old sense of the word. Not like there was, as uncle will tell you, in the last war. Not like when, by com-ing back to London, or even only as far as Paris, you could get, for forty-eight hours, right away from the War—right back into a cush-ioned pre-war life.

To-day the war insists on follow-ing you around, even when you are on leave. On the platform of the London railway terminus it is wait-ing there to meet you; and, as you round the bend of the village main-street, you come face to face with it again. You encounter it in the eyes of your civilian friends. The burr-burr of the telephone in the empty room of the girl who has gone away convinces you. There is no such thing as leave. A fact which the bouillabaisse cannot make you forget, nor the Courvoisier wash away.

All this is not to say that there may not be things that you'll be wanting to do. You may want simply to have "a good time." That can still be arranged.

You may simply be content to spend the days innocent of the button-polishing to which Sir John Simon predestined you, just after the Japs invaded Manchuria in '31.

To have two days away from the spit-and-polish to which Hoare and Laval foredoomed you—five long years ago.

You may be a bit more demanding. You may wish to re-sample the old 1939 way of life. But you can't do that, because it just isn't there any more. Or you may even be really ambitious and want a foretaste of the new life which you hope for, after all this beastliness is over. But there again you're unlucky, because there's no new life budding yet. However you wriggle, you must spend your forty-eight hours in the gap between two worlds.

That's why—though there are parties and pub-crawls, blinds and blondes—there is no such thing as leave.

And that's why, until not only is Hitler totally beaten, but also until a totally new way of life is won, there *can* be no such thing as leave.

*"Mine!"*

"*Yes, this is the Ministry of Information. What do you want to know?*"

# *Progression*

I fell in love with Major Spruce
And never gave a sign.
The sweetest major in the force
And only 39.

It *is* the Major Spruce
And he's grown such a bore,
    such a bore,
I used to think I was in love with
    him.
Well, I don't think so any more.

It *was* the Major Spruce.
He died.   Didn't I tell you?
He was the last of the Spruces,
And about time too.

*STEVIE   SMITH.*

## By Caryl Brahms and S. J. Simon

# F for Ferdinand, 4

THE telephone rang.

Miss Bragg looked at it, laid aside her Proust and stretched out a nicotine-stained finger.

"F for Ferdinand, four," she said toughly.

The three Air Raid Wardens lolling in their deck chairs reached vaguely for their steel helmets. Limbs were still relaxed but they were ready to stiffen at any moment.

"That," announced Miss Bragg in some disgust, "was Report and Control checking the line again."

The wardens relaxed. Miss Bragg noted the time, 04.27, and returned to her Proust.

Wardens Post F for Ferdinand, 4 in the Borough of St. Michael's and All Angels resumed its normal aspect. It looked exactly like *Act I. The Sheriff's Office. Dead Man's Gulch.* But it was in fact in the basement of a block of luxury flats.

The night had been peaceful. Ferdie had been under red since 19 hours but so far there had been no incidents on their sector. The shelters had been quiet, old Mr.

Higginbottom, the patriarch of the part-timers, had providentially fallen asleep in the rest room, and the District Warden had not been near them once. Even Ma from the Buildings appeared to be taking a night off—probably the first for ninety years. She had not once sent our Emmie over to report that something had dropped outside the kitchen window with a mighty thud and would they please send a warden over to see if it was a Molotov.

The telephone rang. Limbs stiffened again. Hands groped for helmets.

"F for Ferdie, four," said Miss Bragg.

The receiver squawked reprovingly.

"Report and Control?" enquired the Post Warden.

"They stink," said Miss Bragg and hung up.

An amiable face peered over the top of a paper. It belonged to Archibald Luke, the kindest-hearted warden in all St. Michael's.

"I would like," he said, "to take

Report and Control, stand them against a wall, and shoot them one by one."

"Take it easy, Mr. Luke," advised the Post Warden. "You've already sat the Civil Service on top of time bombs and bumped off the District Warden. If you don't ration yourself on your murders you'll have no one left to kill to-morrow."

"I'm not on duty to-morrow," said Warden Luke distantly.

Slow footsteps were heard in the corridor. Two wardens were coming in from patrol. One of them was carrying a piece of shrapnel.

"All quiet," they announced. "What about some tea?"

The drone of a plane like a flight of out-of-step bumble bees became audible. Several bangs surrounded it. The drone gathered speed and dwindled.

"Missed him," said Warden Luke regretfully.

They poured out tea. They passed biscuits. They lit cigarettes. Patrick Milligan, the fattest warden, unzipped the top of his siren suit and beamed.

"The big grey car's been around again," he said.

"Why didn't you stop it?" demanded Warden Luke sharply.

"It was going too fast," explained Warden Milligan well pleased.

The Post Warden sucked his pipe thoughtfully.

"Shoot at his tyres," said Warden Luke. "That's what you ought to have done."

Warden Milligan's beam became broader. "No gun," he said smugly.

The big grey car had been providing Ferdie with its light relief for the week. It made a pleasant change from stirrup pumps, searching for delayed-action bombs and Ma from the Buildings. It stood for Mystery.

What was a big grey car doing whizzing round the squares every time there was an air raid? With what object? Ferdie 4 asked itself passionately.

"I think," said the Post Warden, "I might have a word with the District Warden about it."

The suggestion was not well received.

"The District Warden stinks," said Miss Bragg.

The door opened. The District Warden came in. The Post looked at him unhappily.

Colonel Griffiths was a Sahib. But he realised that during the war he would have to make

sacrifices, so he began by treating everybody as an equal.

"Tea again," he said disapprovingly. "Who's on patrol?"

"We are," said two wardens and went.

The Post Warden looked up from filling his pipe.

"We're rather interested in a car," he began.

"Good God," said the District Warden. "What sort of a car?"

"A grey car," said Miss Bragg.

"It whizzes around," explained Warden Milligan.

"In air raids," said the Post Warden. "Regularly. We can't think what it's up to."

"Good God," said the District Warden again. He considered the matter. He plied them with piercing questions. He considered again.

"This is serious," he decided. "We'll have to tackle the job systematically. Tell you what I'll do."

Ferdie 4 waited agog.

"I'll go into it to-morrow," announced the District Warden, yawning slightly. "Only got six hours' sleep last night," he told them, groping for sympathy.

The Post, who for the past fortnight had been averaging two hours, could find no comment.

The District Warden sank into a deck chair. "Wake me up if anything happens," he said.

Ferdie 4 sighed.

"I hear," tempted Miss Bragg, "that they've got a Lilo at Ferdinand three."

The District Warden shook his head. "They don't like me there," he said regretfully.

\*     \*     \*

Time passed. The barrage got louder and louder. Ma from the Buildings got an attack of her old trouble and Report and Control got an attack of the mumbles. But Ferdie 4 continued to function. Miss Bragg still sat at the telephone, now reading Bertrand Russell, the Post Warden discovered a new brand of tobacco, and Warden Luke having blithely swept away the entire High Command in a wishful-thinking earthquake was

now turning his attention to the Vichy Government. And, like a thread of gold romance, the big grey car, untraced and unstopped, whizzed through Ferdie's nights.

But this time all the five posts which formed F district were on the look-out for it.

Colonel Griffiths was not the kind of District Warden to tackle a job systematically and give up in the middle of it. He travelled from post to post, asking piercing questions and leaving strict instructions that he was to be telephoned whenever the big grey car had been sighted. This made a lot of work for Miss Bragg between eight and midnight, in fact one Sunday evening not less than three cars belonging respectively to High Command, the Ministry of Information, and the B.B.C. (the last carrying a popular Postcript to Portland Place) had been held up by eagle-eyed wardens on patrol.

"But we'll get him yet," promised Colonel Griffiths grimly, collapsing into a deck chair at Ferdie 4.

The telephone rang.

"F for Ferdinand, Four," said Miss Bragg. She was always careful of her consonants when the District Warden was listening.

The receiver squawked. Miss

bragg looked excited.

"It's Warden Luke," she announced. "He's just seen the big grey car heading this way."

"Good God," said the District Warden and dashed out, followed by old Mr. Higginbottom.

Warden Luke came in, a smoking service revolver in his hand.

"Shot at his tyres," he announced. "Turned out to be a taxi," he added, regretfully.

The big grey car was not caught that night. Nor indeed for many nights. The pursuit grew hotter. The Police were notified, the Home Guard warned, and even Report and Control stopped checking the line to send an official message.

"All Wardens," they announced at Dictation speed, "should be instructed to be on alert while on patrol during red. They should keep a keen look-out for a big grey car. . . ."

At this point Miss Bragg let out a bellow.

"It's our car," she said fiercely. "You'd never have heard of it but for us. Good-bye."

There was a commotion in the passage. Old Mr. Higginbottom, flushed and panting, trundled into the post. Ferdie 4 looked at him in astonishment. They had not heard an H.E. dropping anywhere.

"Express message," he gasped.

They handed him a pad of coloured forms. Mr. Higginbottom waved them away.

"I've got his number," he croaked. "At least most of it."

He held out a slip. On it was scrawled EXL 246 . . .

They looked at him in awe.

Old Mr. Higginbottom told his story. He told it well. Shorn of its graphic details it appeared that the big grey car had whizzed past him and pulled up at a traffic light.

"I wonder," mused Miss Bragg, "if it's a secret radio guiding Jerry."

"I'll give them radio," said Warden Luke, rising to his feet and patting an ominous bulge in his pocket.

"Luke," cried the Post Warden sharply.

But Warden Luke had already gone.

It was a busy night in the

Borough of St. Michael's. Jerry seemed to be picking on it specially and though all his incendiaries were being put out with an almost contemptuous ease by our devoted A.R.P. services, he kept on sending his planes over with fresh supplies. Report and Control, which for reasons of its own—probably a betting competition—liked to keep track of fires fallen but not started in the vicinity, kept ringing back to make quite sure Ferdie Four had counted correctly, while Ma from the Buildings sent our Emmie over with a strict reminder that if the young men were not over soon she'd throw water on that bomb herself. The shelters were restless. While disinclined to believe the alarmist who was certain they had been burnt to the ground already they decided to play safe and sent a Shelter-Marshal over to make sure.

On top of this there was the big grey car. Now that every man on the sector was busy with stirrup pumps the District Warden had decided that this was the night to catch it. The number was known —most of it anyway—and by to-morrow the cunning blighter would probably have changed it! He whizzed from post to post, nodding briefly at incendiaries,

and urging his men to the hunt.

As the night wore on the pre-occupied hounds got more surely on the scent. Post after post reported that it had sighted the grey car whizzing round the squares.

But it was not till 4.30 a.m. that Warden Luke came into Ferdie 4 brandishing his service revolver.

"Got him," he announced. "Tore his tyres to ribbons. Crashed him into a lamp post."

"What have you done with him?" asked the Post Warden.

"Had to stop to put out an incendiary," apologised Luke. "But our men will pick him up."

"Won't the District Warden be pleased," said Miss Bragg.

There was a sound of footsteps. The District Warden came in. He had a black eye.

"What blasted fool," he snarled, "has been shooting at my tyres?"

There was an awful silence. Warden Luke made for the bathroom. But the Post Warden rose contentedly to his feet. He had got the matter sized up nicely.

"I wonder," he said into the silence, "if your saloon has an EXL number?"

"Good God," said the District Warden.

That night he slept at Report and Control.

*"My thermos flask, it was here a minute ago!"*

As seen by a U.S. dancer

As seen by Stalin

As seen by some
Germans

As seen by Winston
Churchill

**As seen by Roosevelt**

**As seen by Himmler**

**As seen by himself**

**As seen by the Artist**

# INCIDENT

by an A.T.S. Private

# The Girls in Our Squad

THERE was a gang of Cockney girls in our squad. Cockneys can look after themselves all right anywhere, but to our girls it was an art. Before they had been 24 hours in camp, they knew their way around: they knew the time that the last bus left the town, they knew the nearest pubs, cinemas, dance-halls; and they became as beset with boy-friends as marmalade with wasps. They were always first into the cook-house, and first by the fire; they booked the best bunks in the barrack room. They were also first outside on parade, and the corporal in charge of our squad became their champion and mother confessor.

Before seven days had passed, the 30 of us in Room Four had heard all about their labyrinthine love-lives. We knew that they knew a thing or two, which they had found out some time in their teens somewhere in London.

They were strapping, smashing-looking girls. May was big and blooming and blonde; she was the sort of blonde bountiful that the fellows call "Darkie" or "Tiny." If you could have washed the bawdy grin from her face, she would have made a stately beauty.

Daisy, her pal, was as pale and lovely as a Burne-Jones beggar maid: 'woman's weekly' green eyes had she, and clouds of dark hair. She looked cool and quiet, but, corblimey, she was not.

There was Eve as well, who looked like a little angel, but she was very earthy, indeed. Then there was Eve's friend, whose name no one ever knew, and who was the gang stooge, Boots, Buttons, Nurse-maid, Yes-girl, and who was chief safety-pin, suspender and hairgrip-lender in moments of military emergency. She shook us all by finding a steady boy in two days' time. He actually wanted to marry her, which showed that he had some sense.

And there were two or three more in that crowd—all rather tough and tart.

They said that May had worked in a factory, and that Daisy had been a waitress, but, like foreign legionaries, we didn't ask each other about the past. May, Daisy and the rest gave themselves to the Army life with the abandon of wantons, the fervour of novices.

They polished and spat religiously, for to them their kit was sacred, and cleaning it was an act of devotion; marching drill was a ritual, and they were very solemn about it. And when they walked out in the evenings they shone and they swaggered, as smart and as swanky as guardsmen.

Those in our barrack-room who were not of their following hated them very hard. They resented them, feared them, disapproved of them, were disgusted by them, were jealous of them, were attracted to them and hated them.

Those who didn't smoke or drink or swear or use much make-up, the letter-writers and sock-knitters, spent a lot of their time telling each other, tut-tutting, about what May said to-day and what Daisy did.

When the gang came in, a few beers to the bad, and sang "Roll Me Over" with vivid variations, the virginals

became incensed. At times the atmosphere was asthmatic; backchat, bad language, bravura from the gang, would be answered by muted suffering from the spiritual section.

The coming of Christmas didn't improve matters, for it seemed to make the good girls better and the bad girls worse.

THEN came the night before Christmas Eve. Most of us were in because it was too cold to go out. It was too cold even to go across to the canteen, too cold for anything but bed, and it was cold in bed. Bunched up in black

blankets and greatcoats, we tried to write letters under our sheets, or to read sloppy mags under our pillows, or to eat our cakes from home. The Christmas decorations hung sadly from the ceiling. We were all very quiet.

They were singing frosty carols far away across the square. Through the tinsel sound of voice and cornet came a clumping up the stone stair, the noise of scuffling and of much-muffled laughter. The door was pushed open and in skidded the Cockneys, like streamers thrown at a party.

They knocked against the bunks, they slipped on the lino, they sat flat out on the floor. They foamed on to their bunks again, overflowed on to the floor again, moaning, groaning, shouting, screaming, laughing, crying.

We shivered and felt sick and crept under our blankets, and the Pharisees waxed fierce, saying: "Shut up!" and "Disgusting!" and "Ought to be ashamed of themselves!" and "They're getting worse and worse." "They're a disgrace to the A.T.S." "They ought to be kicked out," and "Just wait till

the Orderly Sergeant hears them."

At last the hubbub dissolved into a few hiccoughs and giggles, and they tried to find their way into bed. They got lost and swore.

May was the only one left, still fully dressed, and sitting on her bunk. She was sitting on her bunk and laughing her life away. But then she wasn't howling with laughter any more, but she was just howling. It was a hoarse, barbaric howl, horrible to hear. We had to listen to it even though it hurt us. We held our breath and lay still so as to hear what words she was howling.

"Where's my mother?" she was saying, "I want my mother! I want my mother! Why did God take my mother away? Why did He take her away? Everybody gets letters, but I don't get any letters—no letters from my mother. I want a letter from my mother. Oh, mother, come back to me."

It was as if her pain was in her body and not in her heart.

"My little brother was torpedoed. God, why did You take him away? Why did You kill him? My lovely little brother . . ."

We were all in tears by now and were crying with her in chorus. Eve's friend got out of bed and was shaking her to make her stop. Most of us were just sobbing into our pillows.

In came the Orderly Sergeant.

It was our own Corporal who was on duty that night. She wasn't at all angry. She just tried to comfort her, too. She put May's head on her shoulder and rocked her to and fro.

"Come on now, May," she said, "you mustn't cry. You mustn't cry. You can have my mother. She'll write to you, I promise. I'll tell her to write you a letter and you'll have a lovely parcel for Christmas. My mother will be your mother, too. There, isn't that nice? You mustn't cry, you know. You're in the Army. Dry your eyes and go to sleep and don't forget—you've got a new mother now. Go to sleep like a good girl."

May was a good girl and she was a good soldier.

She said, "I'm sorry, Corporal. Forgive me, Corporal. I didn't mean it. Please don't be angry with me, Corporal."

And she started to weep all over again with the sorrow of being sorry.

At last there was only a whimper and Corporal put out the light.

Next morning no one mentioned it. We did not know for certain if we had not been dreaming.

Yet no one was ever heard to say a hard word to May again, and they picked her out to be marker on our passing-out parade.

And that ended the first lesson of our new life in the Army.

*"Tell me, why do you feel so suited for the 'Wrens'?"*

# OPINION

**By Kathleen Hewitt**

# What They Say About Their Rations

## Landlady:

Half my rooms are empty, but I'm giving my top-back notice. She's bought herself a pair of scales.

## Chorus Girl:

I've got a *real* sugar-daddy who's got diabetes and daren't touch it himself.

## Vegetarian:

I'm leaving for the South Seas, where I shan't be asked what I do with my meat coupons.

## Glutton:

There'll be trouble if they find out, but after all five different names and addresses only just keep me going.

## Butcher:

Some of them think I've got the whole of Smithfield hidden under the counter.

## Doctor:

Neurasthenics never miss an opportunity, and I'm attending quite a crop of pseudo-anæmias.

## Grocer:

Robert Taylor thinks he's been mobbed, but he ought to be here when the news goes round that I've got an extra few pounds of butter.

## Profiteer:

After all, one can always make up on caviare.

## Scientist:

With all my experience in analysis I have only just begun to regard the sausage as a subject.

## Schoolboy:

Grown-ups aren't always a washout. My mother's taken a dislike to butter and I get her whack.

## Schoolgirl:

At least, when I'm a film star, I shan't be another Mae West.

## Professor:

I used to boil my spectacles for four minutes and even the rims suffered, so perhaps the shortage of eggs is a blessing.

*"You'll not find my equal at reconstituting dried egg, ma'am!"*

### Charlady:

If my old man was to see the winks I give the butcher, it'd be a proper triangle drama.

### Cook:

They want a conjurer in the kitchen, and then they'd complain because a rabbit out of a top-hat wasn't a sirloin of beef.

### Restaurateur:

Is it me that like to refuse the good client? I demand of you, Did I make a conflict? In Soho we are all neutral.

### Waiter:

I may have flat feet but my eyes are all right. She ordered steak and handed me half a bus ticket so I gave her beans.

### Ascetic:

I never registered for rationed foodstuffs. Biscuits and boiled water are far more sustaining.

### Wife:

I always remember to smile across the counter, but I've never wangled an extra ounce of anything. And still my husband grudges £40 for a face-lift.

### Husband:

My wife ought to be glad when I'm kept at the office, because by the time I get home I've lost my appetite.

### Exquisite Youth:

I give my bacon coupons to my man. I simply expire if I see anything but aspirin and tea in the morning.

### Gay Girl:

I read an article by a gossip writer or perhaps it was a clergyman, it said that people who drink champagne don't suffer from undernourishment, so I mean to say why *worry* about rations?

### Hamburg Radio Announcer:

Crowds are storming the Corner House of Commons in Great Britain. Cannibalism is rife. Mr. Winston Churchill is marked down as a mouthful for the consumption of Cabinet-makers.

*"It needs absolutely no sugar, no eggs, no fats, no fruit and no milk —*
*and, of course, it's not particularly nice."*

SUSCHITZKY

*So long as there's a chance of learning something, one ought to listen*

TONE                                                                    LONDON

*The number of small pigs from which small legs may be cured will not exceed the average*
*number of small pigs from which only legs were cured in 1936–38*
*Agriculture Minister Sir R. Dorman–Smith explains his bacon policy*

*Peace*

*War*

TOPHAM

*Peace and . . .*
*Hop-pickers 1936*

. . . *War*
*Hop-pickers 1940*

BRASSAÏ

*Blackout in Paris*
*The Moulin Rouge*

## by Peter de Polnay

# A Day in Nazi Paris

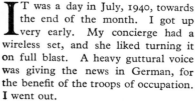

IT was a day in July, 1940, towards the end of the month. I got up very early. My concierge had a wireless set, and she liked turning it on full blast. A heavy guttural voice was giving the news in German, for the benefit of the troops of occupation. I went out.

The Place du Tertre, perched with many trees and much foliage on the top of Montmartre, was still deserted. But on the other side of the square a grey motor-car stood waiting. I thought it was waiting for an officer; for German officers in Paris often stayed out at night—to have a little fun ; in the Parisian manner. It did not occur to them that the ladies they found with such ease were probably anything under the sun but Parisiennes. For even as early as July, 1940, France was resisting through her women.

I was right! A fat, middle-aged officer came from the nether regions of Montmartre. By now I knew his type. The man of the last war, with the memory of his Emperor obliterated from his mind, and love of the Fuehrer burning in his fat, Teutonic heart. A ragged man stopped him and offered to sell him picture postcards of the sights of Paris. The officer asked him if he had any dirty pictures on him. The man had not. The officer turned away and went into Joe's Bar.

At that time I was selling water-colours to the Germans in Joe's Bar, in order to keep seven people from starving. (One of the seven was my Skye terrier, Dodo.)

I went in after the German. I needed money, yet I was angry with him for having come so early to the Butte. For I hated peddling; I usually postponed it till the evening. But, as I've said, I went after him.

He was drinking beer and Benedictine. The German belly is a good mixer. While he drank he gazed into nothingness. Then he asked for note-paper and affably explained to the bar-keeper that he wanted to write to his dear wife and three dear children. He wrote his letter; a benevolent, marital smile followed the antics of his fountain pen.

I was perspiring and feeling hot and cold like any small boy before his exam. In a matter-of-fact voice I asked him if he was interested in water-colours. I was, I added, a Montmartre Kunstmaler. A lie of course, but the Germans bought water-colours if they thought they were dealing directly with such an esoteric creature as a painter. Anyway, one must lie to them. They are made like that.

"Have you any smutty photographs?" he asked, looking up from his letter. In an indignant voice I assured him that I was a painter. He apologised, the result of my indignant voice.

"Do you hang your paintings at the Salon?" he asked.

"Of course," I said. (Oh shades of Segonzac!) So he bought a small water-colour depicting the Madeleine.

"If I come back from England I'll buy an oil painting from you," he said, and I sent up a fervent little prayer that he should not buy an oil painting.

He mused a bit.

"The English will soon be beaten," he said; "it'll be all over in a month." He was quite certain of that.

With the enemy's hundred francs in my pocket I left the bar. Seven mouths would be fed that day.

I looked at the sky. It was grey. My charwoman was coming across the square. I waited for her and then gave her the key of the flat.

"Bad weather again," she said. "So they can't start to-day."

"No," I said, and we both added, "*Dieu soit loué!*"

From the Church of Saint Pierre a grey column was descending towards the square. The first conducted tourist party of the morning. They came along with their boots turning the cobbles into thunder. They sang of their victorious entry into England. They were men of the S.S. Their officer dismissed them outside the Mère Catherine. They rushed into the bars and ordered beer and sausage. But there was little beer left in Paris. After a lot of cursing and arguing they settled down to drinking liqueurs with their sausages. The sausages of Paris, geographically speaking, had travelled a lot at that period. From Strasbourg sausages they had turned into Frankfort sausages. The Germans would soon be drunk.

Coaches loaded with troops began to arrive. Sausages and liqueurs were their goal. Now and then military police put in an unwelcome appearance. They stopped officers and men. But all and sundry had passes. For the Fuehrer had promised that every German soldier of the battles of Flanders and France would see Paris. The only promise that truthful man had kept.

In that obscene grey sea the trees and benches of the square were quite lost. On the fringe at odd intervals dark dots flitted by. The women of Montmartre coming back from the market.

I saw the market in the afternoon when I went down to Paris. It was in the Rue des Abbesses, which is the frontier line of the Butte Montmartre. Food was still to be had, but the potatoes were gone. Germans are partial to potatoes. Outside a butcher's a small queue waited. A woman I knew was in that queue. She was middle-aged and her husband was a prisoner of war in Germany. I stopped to talk to her.

"No potatoes, no butter and no oil," she said. "The Germans say it is on account of the English blockade." She looked round; she dropped her voice. "If only it were true! I wouldn't mind starving if they starved too." Now her voice was a whisper.

"My sister lives at Tethel. The Royal Air Force has bombed the town. Isn't it excellent news?"

At that moment the butcher closed the door of his shop. He put up a notice. "*Plus de Marchandise.*" The

queue dispersed.

"Isn't it excellent news?" my friend repeated, and smiling happily she walked away. Her empty shopping-bag dangled at her side.

I took the Metro at the Place Pigalle. In the station there were many notices in German. Most of them exhorted German soldiers not to hob-nob with the French population, and not to sit on bar stools. Apparently bar stools are un-German. Three cheers for bar stools. The majority of the people of Paris kept to the letter of the instructions for German soldiers. In the Paris Metro there are first and second class coaches. German soldiers travelled free, therefore the French crowded the second class coaches. I remember that a friend of mine, as a mute protest, used to buy a first class ticket and then travel second.

I got out at the Madeleine. The Rue Royale was full. German officers, German soldiers and German civilians.

German cars and lorries rolled on the asphalt. In the Place de la Concorde the statue of Alsace was gone and a German military band was playing in the square. They were playing the *Pilgerchor* of *Tannhäuser*. A few idlers listened. The band stopped. A few seconds later it burst into the *Fallschirmjaegermarsch*. The Champs Elysées opened up before me. It was somewhat dusty under the overcast sky. German cars everywhere, and as I came to it the Arc de Triomphe appeared dark and lifeless, as though the essence of its stones was gone.

When I got nearer I saw coaches and numberless cars parked round the arch. Hundreds of German soldiers stood there gaping, photographing and buying souvenirs from the horde of hawkers.

The wreath the Hun had put on the tomb of the Unknown Soldier on the day of occupation had disappeared. It was better like that. A German sergeant was slowly reading out the names on the arch. Marengo, Austerlitz, Jena and all the others. It took him a long time.

A little, old *camelot* with a tray laden with little Eiffel Towers stood there listening to the guttural notes. He focussed his bloodshot eyes on me and said, "There is still one more name to come there . . . Paris. Perhaps sooner than we expect it." Then he got frightened at his own temerity and ducked into the crowd of gapers.

I went my way. My dog was sick. I bought her some medicine, and returned to Montmartre. The noise and drunkenness of the afternoon were slowly handing over to the noise and drunkenness of the evening. More cars, more Germans, more liqueur and more Frankfort sausages. The bands in the restaurants were playing waltzes from Vienna.

I stood that night outside the Sacré Cœur, and, as was my habit, I looked down on Paris shrouded in the thorough German blackout. But somewhere near the Opéra a single rebellious light dared the darkness. As a matter of fact all the hope of the world centred for me in that light. You can, after two years, still find that light in my cupboard.

by **Paul F. Jennings**

# Moses was a Sanitary Officer

HAVE you ever watched a soldier marching, and wondered what he was thinking about? If he is a species known as A Young Soldier, I can tell you! He is thinking about a little booklet, excitingly titled "Army Form B.51."

I don't know whether they would let civilians have a copy, but if you want one you can try at H.M. Stationery Office, giving them the reference (799) Wt. 25958—1000. 600M. 9/39. W. C. & S. Ltd. Gp. 394. T.S.9825. Forms/B/51/25. And don't forget the (799) or they'll probably give you a Dehospitalisation (Other Ranks with Ague) Certificate instead.

Whoever wrote Army Form B.51 believes in Applied Psychology. The idea is that we should go around muttering health slogans, such as: " . . . my usefulness depends on the state of my feet" or " . . . my skin is a covering for getting rid of waste in the form of sweat." "Hard clean feet" seem to have fascinated the author: feet occur everywhere, like a theme in music. "Flies," he says, "carry minute portions of filth on their feet."

As a matter of fact, I am rather saddened by this. I had always imagined that flies did things conscientiously: I used to imagine them carrying little sacks labelled FILTH over their shoulders and emptying them with a smirk on to the butter. But

they only do it unintentionally with their six little feet.

A.F.B.51 gives Young Soldiers the funniest reasons for doing or not doing things. "*The spittle or saliva is intended to keep the mouth soft . . . such substances as bread, biscuit, rice and pastry require to be well mixed with this saliva . . . in order that they may be perfectly digested. By the habit of spitting you waste this useful substance.*"

On page 6 it says, "*If you feel too much air or draught in a room, wear your woollen cap.*" I like to think of the Young Soldiers sitting on their beds, waiting for Lights Out, looking like goblins in their woollen caps.

But the climax occurs on page 20:—
"*At night it is very important to protect the belly by extra covering. If no blankets are available, any improvised covering will do, such as a belt, an old bag, some straw or a puttee.*"

I dislike the scornful implication of "*an old bag.*" That's right, any old thing will do for these Young Soldiers. Keep those extra blankets and the nice new bags for the sergeants' bellies, and afterwards, perhaps, you might dig up some straw, or a puttee for them.

I would like to tell the bit about Moses being "*an able sanitary officer,*" but I haven't got time. I am off to the Q.-M. Stores on my hard clean feet to get one of those Woollen Caps.

# DISCIPLINE

The Rations Joke—*Cheese-day at the mousetrap*

by Walter Goetz

## What Germans May Laugh At

THE only good jokes in Germany today are those that have to be whispered.

Dr. Goebbels knows that a form of humour is necessary, even to a totalitarian state, but his attempts to make the "German funny men" produce a brand acceptable to the Nazi régime have proved singularly unsuccessful.

The essence of most humour is an element of criticism, and since, in an ideal Nazi State, there should be nothing at which to poke fun, the cartoonists are handicapped from the start. To suggest, for example, that a train was late would be tantamount to saying that Hitler couldn't run a railroad.

While insisting on the general rule that there must be no suggestion of anything wrong in the best of all possible Governments, Dr. Goebbels has been obliged to alter his tactics as the war progresses. For conditions are changing so much for the worse that everyone is aware of them. So he has ordered that some previously unmentionable topics are now to be used, and treated along certain definite lines.

The Black Market Joke—*"Mr. S. had a funny dream last night about a special telescope to convince his customers that nothing is sold under the counter"*

The Air Raid Joke, very daring—*"That was a great chap, murdered seven women." "Is that all?" "Yes, but in those days they had no R.A.F."*

The food situation, for instance: at first there were no jokes at all, then self-conscious titters at the absence of coffee crept in. Now the potato shortage and the black market have become subjects that may—in fact *must*—be mentioned. A joke about the black market has only one purpose—to make the black marketeer despicable in the eyes of his fellows.

## Attacking the Shirkers

When the last extra blanket and woollen sock are collected from people living in unheated houses, there must never be any suggestion that there is something wrong with the army equipment. The cracks are directed at those who are lacking in enthusiasm for the latest "voluntary" hold-up scheme. The cartoonist is, in fact, supposed to shame the public into more patriotic behaviour.

Another object in coming out into the open with something which is common knowledge is to create the impression that the Government is fully aware of the situation, is tackling it bravely, and above all is being truly democratic in allowing it to be mentioned. But when the situation is one where no amount of "shaming" the public will do the trick, then Goebbels reverts to the old method of "see no evil, hear no evil, speak no evil."

Air raids are the perfect example. Apart from a few feeble blackout jokes, or educational ones about rudeness in air raid shelters (as well as one or two "pilloryings" of the brutal R.A.F. for killing exclusively women and children) there has not been a suggestion from any German cartoonist that bombs *can*

The Anti-Churchill Joke

The Political Pornography Joke — *"Don't be frightened, Britannia, he only wants to protect you!"*

fall on a German town.

Any pictorial representation of the Leader, the Government or the high-ups in the armed forces is forbidden, apart from idealised portraits and heavily censored photographs.

Another subject that has to be handled gingerly is the Army. It must not even be hinted that sergeant-majors can be vicious or colonels peppery, or that such things as brass hats exist in the Wehrmacht. All military jokes are made at the expense of civilians, i.e., the raw recruit.

## Belittling the Allies

Thus, having made it impossible for any self-respecting cartoonist to comment intelligently on home affairs, Goebbels lets loose this embittered individual on the "enemy," and here no limits are set to his venom. The result is that, with rare exceptions, the venom is put on so thick that you can't

taste the humour.

"The bigger the lie, the better the lie" is the maxim the boys are told to follow; a hit below the belt counts two. The chap fighting Germany is always an out-and-out villain, and so the picture the German is to have of him must be crude and simple. The aim is to create a kind of sordid, highly-coloured Punch and Judy show.

Whereas we British almost unconsciously tend to differentiate between our enemies—and thus often fall into Axis booby traps such as the story that Goering and the generals really represent the "moderate" Germans—the Germans are precluded from the same tendency by this "nutshell" technique. The only difference admitted between the United Nations is that whichever one is momentarily the most dangerous comes in for the most mud-slinging. But the quality of the mud never varies.

Germany's enemies have invariably certain characteristics in common. It is they who started the fight (and in the last war, as Germany began to lose, it was they who turned down Germany's "reasonable" peace offers). To-day all anti-Axis nations, whether plutocratic or Bolshevik, share the wish to destroy what Germany holds dear—German Socialism or, as the case may be, German ownership of private property —and the reason for this common wish, namely, that they are all ruled by Jews.

A simple device to make the enemy appear weaker is to insist that no really homogeneous united front against the Axis exists, since all parties are acting from purely selfish motives. The argument that England was fighting to the last Frenchman was very successful when applied in direct propaganda to France. The same device has been used against Anglo-American co-operation, and now "the mixture as before" is being applied to our alliance with Russia.

In anti-American propaganda, the last-war cliché that America reacts only to money was brought up to date by Lease-Lend, to show that Churchill is being forced to sell out the British Empire to Wall Street sharks. Roosevelt is only waiting for the day when he can don King George's crown. Unfortunately, this clashes with the argument that Stalin is also waiting for the day when Cripps will open the back door of Buckingham Palace for him.

The U-Boat Campaign Joke—*Wonderful idea of an American inventor; a trap-door in the bottom, so that the valuable ship needn't sink with its precious cargo. The ship stays in harbour and opens the trap-door.*

Here, then, is the picture the ideal propaganda stooge will have of his main enemies. First, England: a decadent plutocracy, the majority of its population living in filthy slums, working for a starvation wage—preferably as children in mines. When its ruling class isn't on horseback shooting foxes, it is firing Indians from the mouths of cannon.

Owing to an appalling blunder of history, the English and not the Germans own half the world. This backward race of island tyrants is ruled over by the arch-villain Winston Churchill. According to the already mentioned recipe, there cannot be a united front anywhere against Hitler; so it is only Churchill and his few friends in the House of Lords who are really interested in prolonging the war. The British, downtrodden cretins that they are, would really welcome the Fuehrer as their deliverer, were they not so poisoned by hate propaganda. Apart from Lords and slum-dwellers, the population of England is Jewish.

America: population Red Indians, negroes, gangsters and—Jews. Rulers

The Unfailing Anti-Semitic Joke—*Mr. and Mrs. Roosevelt worship at the shrine of Jewish capital.*

—the Jewish Mr. and Mrs. Roosevelt. He, an embittered cripple, she, a nymphomaniac. As in the last war, Uncle Sam's main interest is money. But whereas in the last war Wilson was in the pocket of Morgan and Rockefeller, now the financial interests are all Jewish. A comparison of the Uncle Sam of 1917 and of to-day shows that his nose has become progressively more crooked and his hair more curly.

Since pornography is a necessary ingredient of Nazi political humour, sex and crime also play an important part in the life of the country; Hollywood and New York offer convenient scenes for this. The American Army is an inefficient gangster rabble, and American ships are invariably at the bottom of the sea.

Russia: a vast country, inhabited by a horde of sub-human Asiatics— and Jews. It is ruled by an inefficient, vodka-drinking villain who would have spread death and destruction over the whole of Europe had not the Fuehrer started his crusade to save that Continent in the nick of time. The Russian armies consist of press-ganged moujiks, backward and cruel, who only fight because they know their Jewish commissars would shoot them in the back if they didn't, and because their lives are so miserable that they don't care if they die.

Perhaps one should be grateful to the Nazis for the grand job they are doing for us in misleading their own people. The state of delusion in which the Germans are living is a delayed-action bomb; when it goes off it will blow them sky high.

In the meantime there is a cheering comparison to be made between our reaction to world events and theirs. Perhaps the answer to the question: "Will the Germans stand up to bombing as well as the British?" is that during the worst blitz every British paper and music-hall had its bomb jokes, while the Germans are still waiting for theirs.

The Anglo-Russian Alliance Joke—*Stalin tries on his new uniform. (But do the readers ever think of Marshal Goering?)*

*"She says she's from the E.N.S.A."*

*Centre forward*

TONE

LONDON

*Captain of the team*
*Field-Marshal Montgomery*

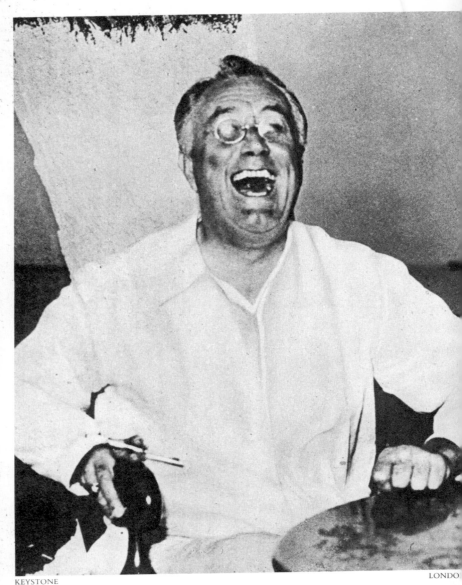

KEYSTONE                                                          LONDO

*"Swing it, baby!"*

*"O.K., Franklin!"*

*America enjoys herself*

*Japan is apprehensive*

WIDE WORLD

LON

*Japanese soldiers*

*Frightened monkeys*

*Animals and men*
*The best animal picture in the world. This neurotic ape, who escaped*
*from his jungle home into the Caribbean Sea, was driven mad by the chatter of*
*female monkeys. The photographer swam a quarter of a mile with the*
*camera strapped to her shoulders to take this picture*

## by Frederich Wolf

# Spring in a Concentration Camp

*April is the cruellest month, breeding*
*Lilacs out of the dead land, mixing*
*Memory and desire, stirring*
*Dull roots with spring rain. . .*

T. S. ELIOT.

"WE have accustomed ourselves to captivity, to the barbed wire, to the whistles of the guards; we have got used to the rifle butts and the punches, the footsteps of the drunken sergeants on Saturdays and Sundays; to the attacks of dysentery and colic for which we are given no medicines. To all of this we have become accustomed. Luckily we have also our language courses, our technical and other lessons, which we carry on despite all difficulties; we conduct a fight against spies and provocateurs, we have ties of comradeship with the other prisoners. We react to every attack, to every danger, to every token of solidarity, to every situation, with the speed of a muscular reflex.

There comes, however, a situation for which we are quite unprepared.

Hitherto the only birds we have seen, during roll-call at dawn and dusk, are the swarms of crows flying from the forest to the fields and back to their nests. They, too, have their regula-tions, their work to carry out, we said. They did not disturb us! Then, one day at noon, in pale sunshine, someone shouts into the barrack room : "Birds are flying over the camp!"

Everybody runs out. Indeed, a long train of twittering black birds is flying from the south to the north. These are starlings "travelling" from Africa over the Mediterranean. A couple of days later come whole swarms of swallows. Often they rest in long chains on our barbed wire. After them come the warm days, the southern winds, in place of the icy Pyrenean blasts and Biscay storms.

In the evening, the three thousand-metre violet peaks of the Pyrenees, still snowclad, stand sharp against the golden western sky. More clearly lies the blue-black zone of the pine forests, still more clearly the delicate green of the leafy woods, and, already visible from the camp, the meadowy slopes begin to blossom in all colours. Through the barbed wire we can easily make out the flowering bright yellow broom shrubs; it almost looks as though, out on the meadows, flaxen-haired women were waiting to meet us.

For this sudden, wonderful, con-founded spring, we are not prepared. Old men begin, for no earthly reasons, to fight each other with wooden stools, until blood flows.

A young Yugoslav, who has been brooding in silence for days, rushes with a knife upon a comrade; he can hardly be quieted. He breaks loose from our grasp, leaps with big strides through the camp, through eight lines of barbed wire, his breeches hanging down in shreds.

The guards open fire, but he dashes through, across the road and into the bushes and out on to the high embankment. There he lies down on the grass, among the flowers, and quietly looks up at the sky.

Panting, the guards run after him, with their guns at the trail; they seize him, doubly bind his arms and legs, and bring him back to the camp.

He smiles quite calmly and says to us: "Oh, it was lovely out there in the open!"

This wonderful, terrible spring! In the evening some of the prisoners sing songs in their native tongues—Spanish, Russian, Italian, German—others run to the far end of the camp and shut their ears.

Again and again single prisoners, or whole groups, try at night to crawl through the barbed wire. And again and again shots are heard and the alarming cries of the guards bringing back through the barbed wire trap a would-be runaway, gasping desperately, half bleeding to death, perhaps unconscious already.

We have our hands full trying to keep discipline among ourselves, trying to strengthen ourselves in the fight against the spring. We set our teeth and go on with our courses, we organise evening sports and choir concerts.

We battle against the spring, against longing, against life without women. And a hard and bitter struggle it is."

*Vernet,* 1940.

*"I haven't told her about the war: she'd only fret"*

*"Three days, and still no sign of rescue"*

By David Low

# The Cartoonist in War

IN one way a cartoonist's work is simplified in wartime because there is only one subject, though, if he be conscientious, there are of course many angles of it with which to deal. The most patient of readers grows bored with constant repetition of the points that the enemy is a fool and a blackguard and that our brave boys will kick his pants.

People know that things are not so simple as all that and they want to know the how, the why, and the when, which means that cartoonists have to be students. When they have to work ahead they have also to be prophets, and to be a prophet these days is no joke. Sometimes I have to draw cartoons to appear in foreign newspapers one month later. Normally one can say fairly well what features of the international landscape will "stay put," so to speak; but how would you like to guess what the situation' is going to be one month hence in these times? If Hitler doesn't do what I think he is going to do I shall have to

eat several cartoons. I may say that I have taken long chances on that fellow and haven't had to eat one yet. Perhaps it's because we're both artists.

There used to be an established technique for drawing war cartoons. The cartoonist made pictures of British lions, Russian bears and German eagles striking attitudes, and saying things like "Bravo, little Belgium!", "England is proud of you!" or "This must not go on, sir!" to each other.

But this is all so foreign to the spirit of to-day as to seem like fairy-tale stuff. The British lion and so on are now obsolete junk. And so are Britannia, Germania, La Belle France and all of those statuesque females in Greek nightgowns who symbolised the imperialisms in the cartoons of our fathers. That is, unless you hold that the present war is one between rival imperialisms, in which case I should disagree with you. R.I.P. to the Britannia stodge, I say. And also to John Bull, that symbol of smug, narrow patriotism, with whom the average modern Briton has nothing whatever in common. If you think that this average Briton is facing this war in that spirit and preparing to fight for, rather than against, what that kind of thing represents, let me tell you that you are making a pretty considerable mistake.

In past wars, too, cartoonists used to run to what were called "powerful" cartoons: horrific scenes of mangled mothers and children, plenty of blood and bones. No doubt drawing cartoons of that kind gave—and

gives—relief to the cartoonist; it helps to get surging emotions out of the system. But whatever their popular appeal may have been in past wars, they do not get across in this one. The present generation may admire the artistry of the composition, but it is unmoved by the trite statement that war is horrible, because it knows that only too well already. The movies and the newsreel have hardened it to visual horror. In looking at his cartoons the average man or woman of to-day is more analytical and wants to savour arguments and to appreciate where the sense of things lies.

Moreover, the horrific cartoon is not an effective political approach in this war. No dictator in these days is inconvenienced or even displeased by cartoons showing his terrible exercise of power or his terrible person stalking through blood and mud. That is the kind of idea about himself that a

*The light in my studio is dimmed by cellophane. . . .*

THE SCOURGE OF MANKIND

?

*Hitler likes to be drawn like this —*                                    *— but not like this*

power-seeking world-beater would want to propagate. It not only feeds his vanity, but unfortunately it shows profitable returns in an awed world. What he does not want to get around is the idea that he is an ass, which is really damaging.

I shall always remember Hitler, for instance, not as the majestic, monstrous myth of his propaganda build-up, but as the sissy who whined to the British Foreign Office about his dignity when I ran him for a while as a comic strip.

If you believe, as I do, that human personalities are the fitting symbols of the policies they represent, the personalities involved in the war are not a bad bunch to draw. The principal boy, so to speak—Hitler—is not, however, the best of his side.

If I had been asked to choose a picturesque war lord, I should have had a big dark scowling man. Hitler has the will to be picturesque, but whatever you do with his face his physiognomy is essentially weak to draw, probably because Hitler is a mixed type—unlike the Nordic type of Goering or the Mediterranean of

Goebbels. One of my difficulties about Hitler is that I have to use fine lines to draw his eyes, and when I send cartoons by radiogram to foreign countries the transmission process cannot pick up all these lines and my Hitler arrives at the other end with the eyes lost on the way. Goebbels, on the other hand, is good to draw—dark, sharp lines. As a citizen of the world I should not think it an improvement, but as a cartoonist I don't mind how soon Goebbels purges his friends and makes himself Public Enemy No. 1.

Stalin is good; or rather, should I say, Stalin's moustache is good, because the background is secondary. That moustache would dominate any landscape. On the strength of the moustache Stalin has established himself as a horrific superman in cartoons so successfully that one automatically draws him about seven feet high and

broad in proportion. It comes as a shock to see that Stalin is a middle-sized, homely, amiable-looking old gent in real life.

On the Allied front the leaders are good to draw, too: Chamberlain, whose aquiline features in photographs might have earned him the title of the Avenging Eagle, is belied by his features. He falls into lines strongly marked but sad. He is known at the House of Commons as the Undertaker. Though easily drawn, he is a static one-pose man, unlike the volatile Lloyd George of the last war, who in his infinite variety of movement was the caricaturist's joy. Halifax, his lieutenant, has also only one appearance, but a highly picturesque one. Halifax is the foreigner's idea of the horse-faced Englishman come to life.

A cartoonist might complain, however, that the leaders of the democracies are hardly picturesque.

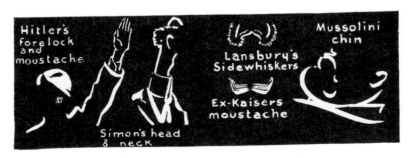

They, not being dictators, have no urgent need to dramatise themselves and depend more on their natural charms. But at the other extreme they probably overdo their dependence on their natural charms and their reluctance to be picturesque. Winston Churchill is a shining exception among the British side, probably because from his earliest political days he has studied his own caricatures and endeavoured to live up to them. Far and away the best actor, he is now the most striking and drawable personality in British public life. "Clothes make the man" is a saw which might be pondered by democratic leaders, perhaps. Daladier is a Napoleonic type—a little sadder—who, if he wore a Napòleon make-up, could put Hitler in the shade. As it is, when I have to draw him I feel that his sack suit is incongruous.

The best man in Europe to draw, of course, is Mussolini, who may be added here as one who sits on the edge of this war. His highly dramatic, if now slightly old-fashioned, ensemble suggests always to me that he ought to wear a credit label: "Produced by Cecil de Mille." With another two feet to his height he would be the wench's dream of a dictator. As

it is, by standing on raised platforms and protruding his chin, which is in reality more fat than he would like to admit, he puts across very well a plausible foundation for the cartoonist's big, burly, truculent figure. As for Ciano, Mussolini's lieutenant, he is just Grandpa Mussolini's copycat. His wife, Mussolini's daughter Edda, knows the business.

Now I am going to my studio to draw. Thanks to Hitler, conditions are not now too happy. One of my troubles is light in

*Churchill! Most drawable personality in British public life*

these black-out days. My studio is all glass on one side, but the light is dimmed by sheets of cellophane stuck on to prevent my becoming a human pin-cushion if I happen to be in when a bomb drops. That in itself is inspiring, though.

At a time like this there is no dearth of material. The indignation generated at the spectacle of man's inhumanity to man always provokes a copious expression in cartoonists, as the sight of a large man kicking a child might provoke you to copious speech. It may sound sententious, but the defence of the decencies of life is part of a cartoonist's business.

The quality that divides—or should divide—the art of a cartoonist from that of the purely humorous artist is that underlying the satire of the former is an implied contrast with something better. A highly moral calling, that of deflating the flocks of humbugs, hypocrites and incompetents that seem always to grow and flourish like the green bay tree in time of war.

That's the more serious side of cartooning. There is the lighter side. The surprise changes and contrasts from yesterday to to-day, however serious their significance, have their lighter aspects.

People walking around with their little gas-mask boxes on their shoulders . . . people with luminous paint medals on their hats in the black-out . . . travellers sitting in trains in the dark staring at one another with cats' eyes . . . sedate suburbanites hopping out of bed and bunging into holes in the ground at the sound of the siren's song . . . the statue of our Charles I buried in sandbags in Trafalgar Square. . . .

You know that our income tax was raised recently to 7s. 6d. in the £.

Would you believe it (money is a serious matter) that, when this was announced by the Chancellor of the Exchequer in his budget, the whole House of Commons laughed. Although I, like everybody else was well and truly soaked, I was pleased.

Part of the cartoonist's social function (but not all of it) is to be a clown which is just as it should be at a time like this.

The strength of the British people is that it can see the joke and purge itself of bitterness in so doing. That, to me, as a student of the psychology of humour, is a test of the greatness of a people.

# What David Low thinks of them

GOEBBELS: "He is good to draw—dark sharp lines."

LLOYD GEORGE: "His variety is the caricaturist's joy."

STALIN: "His moustache establishes him as a superman."

DALADIER: "A Napoleonic type—though a little sadder."

HALIFAX: "The horse-faced Englishman come to life."

CHAMBERLAIN: "He falls into lines strongly marked but sad."

"Hey, you're dead!"
"No I'm not. I'm just sort of staggering forward, weak with
loss of blood and exhaustion, to recapture our position . . ."

## by a Clippie

## "You, My Passengers"

*THIS article arrived at our office with the following letter :—*

Dear Sir, This is my first attempt at writing. I have been 24 last week, come from Czecho-Slovakia, wanted to become actress. Since living in England I have been working in domestic service, have been in a artificial silk mill, learned how to enlarge and print photographs and worked in an El.Eng.Co. making electric soldering irons. The only sane thing about me is that I know that I am a lunatic. I wrote the article coming off late duty at 12.30 at night.

Yours respectfully, *E. Brunner.*
*Manchester.*

I AM only one of those sometimes admired and more often cursed beings called Clippies, by the mob, and guards, or conductresses by higher society. Probably most people will find it below their dignity to read this, but as I have heard Mr. Churchill and various other people say that this is a democracy I'll try my luck and let the public know a bit about us yelling, pushing, money-taking, paper-issuing beings.

The absence of "human" in two of the previous sentences is not accidental, but as you're repeatedly told that you are only a public servant, you become more or, shall I say, less than that, you become a robot.

The average pretty, cheerful and polite conductress has a quite good time in the first and last week of points and personal rationing. I think in those weeks I get about a quarter of biscuits and at least a quarter of sweets and chocolate a week. In the weeks between I get less. I also get about 10-20 cigarettes a week.

People in working class districts are worse than those in so-called, "better quarters" that are as a rule called "snobs." The poorer people will, when they've got it, make you change 2/-pieces and halfcrowns and will swear at you for very little if any reason at all, while the snobs will try to find the money and if they have anything to say will say it with dignity. Nevertheless, I wish some of my passengers could be overheard by their friends. It would be an experience.

Why people cannot move quick is beyond me, why they do not teach courtesy at school is also something which I cannot understand.

The average passenger is nice to you if you're nice to him, but on occasions very stupid, especially when you ask him to move along the passage to make room for additional passengers. But still, with a smile and a joke you might persuade him to do even that and then you're queen of the bus. The other day I was called a "b .... foreigner" by a "gentleman." No, I did not push him off. I only quietly handed my tickets over to him and asked him to take the job over. He did not feel like it so I told him to keep quiet and let me do my job. All very politely and with a smile. That night, I got two bars of chocolate and 20 cigarettes, just because I did not lose my temper. But then I have no worries but I do want to pay a tribute to those girls doing the job, who have a few children and a house to look after. Believe me, they have their

worries and if you meet a conductress, which is not so pleasant, think how you'd feel if your child is ill and you have to go to work.

I've written all this out of an impulse to make the public see us as human beings and also because I love you, my passengers, you charming, idiotic, ungrateful bunch of creatures, who, godlike, smile down upon us and open the door to hell.

In any case, getting up at 5 o'clock in the morning is no picnic.

*"Doesn't anybody know where Miss Cooper puts the key!"*

*"I love every acre of that girl!"*

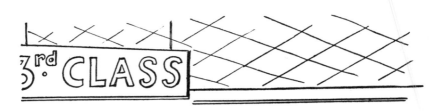

## By Margery Sharp

# Night Engagement

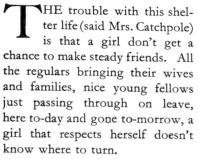

THE trouble with this shelter life (said Mrs. Catchpole) is that a girl don't get a chance to make steady friends. All the regulars bringing their wives and families, nice young fellows just passing through on leave, here to-day and gone to-morrow, a girl that respects herself doesn't know where to turn.

Take my Doris: time and again she's come back to our corner and said, "Mum, there's ever such a nice young fellow just been chatting to me, but he isn't a regular."

"Bring him over," I say, "and let's have a look at him." So she brings him over, and we pass a pleasant evening and then the minute the All Clear goes he says, "It's been a great pleasure meeting you, now I'm off to Aberdeen," and a fat lot of good that is to a girl that lives in S.W.1.

"Take heart, Doris," I say, "there's a Mr. Right somewhere."

"Not in *this* shelter," says Doris, "not for a girl that respects herself; I think I'll try the Tube;" so the next night, off she goes in her siren-suit with half the sandwiches and a bottle of tea.

Well, I don't see her again till next morning when I find her at home in the scullery having a wash before she goes to work.

"Well, Doris," I say, "how's the Tube?"

"Well, mum," she says, "I really can't tell. I met ever such a nice young fellow, works in the Post Office, stood me a cup of coffee and everything, only then a Warden butted in, said I better look out he had quite a name in the shelter and no companion for a girl that respects herself; so I really can't tell."

"Will he be there to-night?" I ask.

"Oh, yes," says Doris, "we made a date after the Warden cleared off."

"Then you better take me along with you," I say, "and let me have a look at him." So that night off we trek, bed and bedding, and there sure enough is Doris's new friend—ever such a nice young fellow, though not so young at that, and not what you'd call delighted to see me.

"Harry," says Doris, "this is Mum."

"Pleased to meet you," I say, "perhaps we may offer you a sandwich?"

"Thank·you very much," says he, "perhaps in return I may offer you a coffee?" And off he goes to fetch it, and we never see him again. Well, Doris blames me, of course, says I oughtn't to have come in my curlers, but what I say is if a fellow's put off by curlers he don't know the facts of life and you're better without him. However, Doris takes umbrage, says she thinks she'll go along to the Fire Station and see if they want a mascot.

Well, she never got there, lucky as it turned out, because they'd an Alsatian dog already, but what did happen was the Blitz got something fierce, Doris popped into a cellar, and down came the whole place on top of her.

Well, I know nothing about it till she doesn't turn up in the morning, and when a girl that respects herself like Doris that means something, so I trot off to the Fire Station (that's when I found about the dog), but they hadn't seen her.

So then I went round and about, and I don't mind telling you I was worried to a rind, and at last I find a whole demolition squad digging Doris out. I know it's Doris because they can hear her voice faint through the ventilator, and they let me creep in to have a chat.

"Are you all right, Doris?" I call.

"Oh, yes, Mum," she says, "there's ever such a nice young fellow down here with me, works on the Railway, and would you believe it, he knows Auntie Flo."

"You bring him along," I say, "and let's have a word with him. So along he comes to the ventilator, and I call down again.

"That's my daughter Doris," I say, "I'm her Mum, and when you get out I'll be very pleased to meet you."

"Mrs. Catchpole," he says, "that goes for me too." So I creep out again and ask the squad how long they'll be at it. They say they can't tell, they'll be as quick as they can; so I say, if there's no danger not to hurry themselves, because it does look as though Doris is on to something at last, though I don't say that last bit aloud, perfect gentleman as the officer was; called me 'Madam' and everything.

Well, I went along and got some cigarettes and made some tea in a bottle and the lady next door very

kindly let me have a tin of salmon and back I went to pass them down to Doris, who says I better go round to her office and tell them she'll have to have the day off.

The squad wasn't looking too happy and the house next door had caved in as well, but Doris says they're still quite okay, plenty of air and no gas, and her new friend had shored up the ceiling with a bedstead they found.

"Best use for it," I think, and as I can't do anything more off I go to the office, very nice about it they were, and then on to my sister Flo.

"Do you know a fellow," I ask, "works on the Railway?"

"What name?" she asks.

"I don't know his name," I say, "but he works on the Railway and

he's buried along of my Doris."

"Well, that's either Ted Parker," she says, "married and three kids, or Arthur Greenway, nice young fellow lives with his Mum."

"Well, let's hope and pray it's Arthur," I tell her, and I think it would be a kind and neighbourly act to go and have a word with Mrs. Greenway, in case she doesn't know what's happened to him. And sure enough she doesn't, worried to a rind she was, and ever so glad to hear he was safe and sound along of my Doris.

We had a cup of tea together, and I took a good look over the house, Mrs. Greenway said Arthur was a teetotaller and Primitive Methodist, didn't go with the girls because he liked them steady and said that to find a girl that was steady was like getting a camel through the eye of a needle.

"Why, he ought to meet my Doris!" I say, and we both have to laugh because of course he *had* met her.

So we have a bit more pleasant chat, and I tell her about Doris, how she was a girl that always respected herself and then off we go together to where they're still digging Doris and Arthur out. A different officer, not a patch on the first, kept telling us to stand back because it was near black-out and if the blitz started there was no knowing what might happen.

"That's all very well," I say, "but that's my Doris down there, and this lady's Arthur, and we want to have a word with them."

"You stand back and have a word with your Maker," he says, really hardly polite.

Well, I don't know about Mrs. Greenway, but as a matter of fact I did do a bit of praying, and it may have been that or it may not, but just as the first Jerries came over one of the men crawled in through a hole and crawled out again dragging Doris after.

Doris had a lot of plaster and such in her hair, but her siren-suit had stood up wonderful.

And young Arthur too, though no beauty, had brought out a cat he found down there, which showed he had a kind nature. Well, by this time we were quite like old friends, so we thanked the squad and the officer, I also sent my best wishes to the first officer and back we went to the Greenways and had some tea.

By this time the blitz was in full swing, so I say to Doris, "Well, Doris, is it to be the Tube or the shelter?"

"Oh, no," says young Arthur, "we've got an Anderson in the yard, you must stay with us."

"That's right," says Mrs. Greenway, "you must stay with us like Arthur says."

"Well, if we don't intrude," I say.

"You must come to us regular," says Arthur, "for I don't like to think of Miss Catchpole in a public shelter; you never know who you may meet."

"Oh, I've never met anyone," says Doris.

"Until last night," says Arthur, with a meaning look; and though maybe he didn't know his fate, I and Doris and his Mum did all right, and it's lucky Mrs. Greenway and me get on so well so the young people can have the place to themselves.

*One of the great artists of our day – Henry Moore in his studio*
*In the following pages we reproduce shelter drawings by the sculptor, Henry Moore, alongside*
*photographs by Brandt. These were made quite independently, in the early part of the 1940*
*blitz, before official shelters had been organised. Obviously no comparison in artistic value is*
*intended; a photograph, however imaginative, is the record of a scene; a work of art sets out to*
*convey the formal and emotional idea behind the scene. We print them together because it seems*
*to us that in this case photographs and drawings increase the appreciation of each other.*

*Liverpool Street extension*
Brandt took this photograph in a disused tube tunnel. "Deep below the ground," he says,
"the long alley of intermingled bodies, with the hot, smelly air and continual murmur of snores,
came nearest to my pre-war idea of what an air-raid shelter would be like."

*Tube shelter perspective*
Henry Moore visited the same shelter just after it was opened. It seemed to him to stretch
for miles, and its inhabitants to have been sleeping and suffering for hundreds of years. The
picture is formalised to give an impression of an infinite number of people, stretching back into
distance. To achieve this the artist has had to simplify the pattern and wipe out much detail.

*Spitalfield Crypt*
*Shelterers moved about by candle-light in what must have been one of London's eeriest shelters.*
*This crippled woman spent her nights in an alcove from which the coffins had been cleared. Her*
*face and attitude show determination, even in sleep.*

*The roman matrons*

The two women, Moore says, were sitting quietly, and stoically accepting their situation; waiting for the night to come to an end. They might have been carved out of stone. Most of Henry Moore's early drawings had been done as designs for his sculptures, and he had never attempted draperies. The clothes of the shelterers gave him a new problem. He would not give them a fashion; he wanted to make his figures timeless, suggesting that, though their situation might be strange, there was nothing new about their suffering.

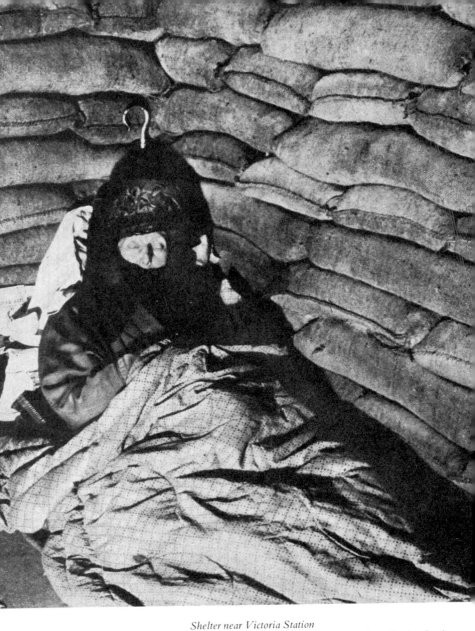

*Shelter near Victoria Station*
*It is interesting to notice how often Brandt and Moore, working quite independently of each*
*other, chose similar subjects for their work . . . "I found this old lady," says Brandt,*
*"in a huge noisy shelter near Victoria. She knew nobody among the crowds and went to sleep*
*early, sitting upright, just as she had arrived. With her umbrella tucked away behind her and*
*her hat tied on with a shawl, she gave her corner a last-century air of decorum and primness".*

*Woman seated in the Underground*

*Among a mass of people forced into each other's company there are usually one or two who contrive to remain solitary. This ghostlike figure was such a one. Her attitude has none of the courage of the " Roman Matrons." She is helpless and pathetic in the tide of events that have brought her here. Moore records her individual emotion, while the people in the background are intended as a reminder that it is a suffering common to all.*

*Pink and green sleepers: a drawing by Henry Moore*
*Henry Moore thinks this shelter drawing is one of the best he has made. He wanted to*
*give the feeling of two people in an uneasy sleep. They are more suggestive of horror than the*
*other sleepers he has drawn. Their attitude, their hands and faces, tell of their apprehension.*
*In this picture the formal and emotional ideas have been welded together into an imaginative*
*whole.*
*When the War Artists' Committee saw the shelter drawings Henry Moore was making, they*
*arranged for him special facilities for visiting the shelters, and they bought for the nation a*
*number of his works, including all those we have printed in this section.*

## By Arthur Koestler

# My Foulest Christmas

*We asked a number of interesting people for their recollections of the foulest Christmas they had ever spent. Here is one reply:—*

THE first night of Christmas, 1931, I spent fully dressed in the pitch dark room No. 308 of Hotel Regina in Kharkov. I shared that bed with a novelist from Kiev, the chied of the local militia of Dnjepropetrovsk, three bottles of vodka, a jar of salted cucumber and a loaf of black rye bread.

We were having a party, and as the temperature in the room was 5 degrees below freezing point, the only solution was to have it in bed.

The population of Kharkov had about trebled during the first five-year plan, and several new factories had been built; the central electric power plant had not been enlarged proportionally, and one after the other the giant steam turbines had burst under the strain; consequently, during all the winter of 1931–32 the capital of the Ukraine was left without electric light, without tramways and without central heating in the buildings operated by electric pumps.

If one smoked in the street the moisture froze in the cigarette end, which became as hard as a stick and gave one the sensation of chewing nicotined ice cream.

We fed and drank and sang in the dark in my bed, and as the bed was narrow and all three of us had vatinkas on—black smocks lined with an inch-thick layer of cotton wool—we kept falling out of it in turns.

The novelist from Kiev lived in the room next to mine and the militia chief, who was also manager of a state - pig - breeding - farm - trust, lived across the corridor. He had come to Kharkov six weeks ago on a *kommandirovka* or official mission, to discover the whereabouts of some waggon-loads of pig-food lost on their way to Dnjepropetrovsk. He had not found them yet. In those days one had to queue up for everything in the Ukraine, and the novelist

217

gave us a lurid description of how the militia chief's three thousand pigs had been queueing up for the last six weeks in the main street, waiting in sorrow for their master's return. This kept us amused for about twenty minutes; then I tried to teach them to repeat very quickly the English words Big Pink Pig, Big Pink Pig. This kept us amused for another twenty minutes.

I forgot to say that there were also three female comrades at my party. They lay, equally in vatinkas, in the second bed, two feet apart from ours. Whenever our vatinkas accidentally touched their vatinkas over the abyss, they squealed like the chief's pigs, and their main contribution to the entertainment was to give the comrade from abroad, that was me, discourses on the new proletarian morality.

In the end we carried the bed with the three shrieking female comrades out into the corridor and locked the door.

The cucumber was frozen and next day I got bronchitis.

"*The lift gains a floor every 24 hours*"

by J. Maclaren Ross

# He Died for His Country

I DIDN'T know he was dead at first. He didn't look dead to me. Big, strapping bloke, hat on the back of his head, leaning against the pub counter drinking a pint. What's more, he'd just bought me one.

"What're you having, mate?" he said, and pulled out a wallet fairly bulging with quid notes. "Another pint, miss. Always glad to buy a drink for anyone in the Army. Ex-soldier meself."

"Get your ticket?" I asked him.

"In a manner of speaking," he said, bending confidentially forward.

"Do you know what?" he said. "You're talking to a dead man."

"A dead man?" I said.

"Straight up," he said. "Honest truth."

"How long have you been dead?" I asked him.

"Ever since Dunkirk," he told me. "That's where I got killed—Dunkirk."

"Were you blown up or just shot?"

"That I couldn't rightly say, mate. Got killed in action, that's all I know. Tell you how it happened. I gets back from Dunkirk, see? Goes to a big kind o' rest camp first of all. Officer there pays me out four quid and gives me a seven-day pass. Off I goes back home to the missus. 'I'm home for keeps,' I tells her. 'I ain't a-going back.' 'What you going to do?' she says. 'Get work,' I says. 'What about identity?' she says,

'you can't get work without you have identity. You only got your Army book,' she says. 'I ain't got that,' I tells her, 'chucked it down the bleeding drain. I'm through with the Army, I am. Civvy from now on.' 'You're crackers, Bert,' she tells me.

"Anyhow, couple o' days later I'm going through one of me old civvy suits and I comes acrost me identity card. I can't have give it up when I went in the Army, see! So off I goes with it to a big munition factory where they needs blokes. They don't arst me no questions, I don't tell 'em no lies. I gets signed on, seven pound a week. Dead cushy."

"Didn't they come after you?"

"They did not. Course, arter I been absent couple o' weeks I expected 'em to. I says to the missus, 'Ethel,' I says, 'I best get digs out, they'll be calling round here right shortly.' 'Right you are, Bert,' she says. So I gets digs close to me work.

"But I ain't been there two days afore the missus come over in the hell of a dooda. 'Here, Bert,' she says, 'look what I got,' and she waves a War Office telegram at me. 'Your husband reported missing, believed killed,' it says. 'Stone a crow,' I says. 'Make a muck of anything they would in the Army,' I says. 'I'm minded to go right back there and chew 'em up about it.' 'Don't you be so foolish, Bert,' she says. 'Can't you see? If they think you're dead you won't never have to go back.' 'There's something in that,' I says. So I stays put, and by and by letter from Records come through saying they're sorry I'm dead. Killed in action. Dunkirk.

"'Well, that's legal,' I says to the missus, 'they can't get round that. I'm dead right enough,' and the missus gets herself all decked out in black straight off. 'We'll get a pension now, Bert,' she says; 'just you keep under cover till it comes through. Widow's pension, see?' And sure enough she did. Extra quid a week for damn all.

"And that's where the trouble starts. She moved out when the pension started coming. 'Ain't safe to stay around here with everyone thinking you're dead,' she says to me. And she goes and gets digs elsewhere.

"Well, she don't come over to see me for going on a fortnight. And what d'you think? She's got another bloke meantime. ' Get out,' she tells me, 'we don't want no dead men around here.' Well, I give it her proper, then. 'Corpse, eh!' I says. 'And me that died for my country, too.' And I gives her a black eye. Then this bloke she got now came out, ruddy civvy, reserved occupation, never done his bit. I didn't 'arf lay into him. Knocked him for six.

"THEN out I goes to the pub and gets proper cut. I'd put away a good few pints and I comes out closing time and bumps bang into an M.P. arresting an absentee. Well, as I say, I'm always ready to help a soldier, so I hauls this M.P. off. 'You let that bloke go,' I says to him. 'Who the hell are you?' he says. 'Never you mind,' I says. 'I do mind,' he says 'Let's see your identity card,' he says. 'I'm dead,' I tells him, 'you can't do nothing to a dead man.' 'What d' you mean, dead?' he says. So I pulls out the letter from Records and shows it him. 'There you are,' I says, 'black and white, official.'

"Up comes another M.P. 'What's the row?' he says. Anyhow, in the finish they run me in, dead man or no dead man. In the morning I wakes up. I thinks, 'that's caused it. Anyhow, they'll stop the wife's ruddy pension, that's one comfort,' I says to meself.

"By and by an escort from me old mob comes to fetch me. Down to Depot. No one I knew there. 'Who're you?' they say. 'I'm dead,' I say. 'All right then, you don't want no ruddy grub,' they say. 'Don't I, by heck,' I says. In the end they give me some bread and cheese. I go before the M.O. 'Dead, eh!' he says. 'Well, I can't do nothing for you.' I come up before the Old Man. He says, 'Dead, are you? Get the hell outa here.'

"So they give me a railway warrant and the letter from Records saying I'm dead, and off I goes back to me job.

"Have another pint? Loan of a quid? Sure, take it. Always ready to help anyone in the blinking Army.

"Oh, and what d'you think? A proper laugh. Copper come round checking up at my digs yesterday. Summonsed me, he did, for having an identity card belonging to a dead man. Got to come up before the beak Monday. Much I care. Nothing they can do, see? Anyhow, I'm not worrying. Why worry? Dogs don't."

*"We're from Oflag 862B5"*

**500 ft.**

**115 hours**

**6 mins. 29 secs.**

# What a Man Can Endure

*It is on record that a man can :—*

| | | |
|---|---|---|
| Live without sleep for | .. | 115 hours |
| Live without water for | .. | 22 days |
| Live without food for | .. | 75 days |
| Hold his breath for.. | | 20 mins. 5 secs. |
| Stay under water for | | 6 mins. 29 secs. |
| Live in a heat of .. | .. | 120° C. |
| Live in a cold of .. | .. | −75° C. |
| Withstand noise of .. | .. | 130 decibels |
| Glide for .. .. | .. | 465½ miles |
| Climb without oxygen to | .. | 28,200 feet |
| Climb with oxygen to | | 74,000 feet |
| Dive below water to | .. | 500 feet |
| Run (in 59 days) .. | .. | 5,625 miles |
| Walk on his hands 16 miles per day for | .. .. | 55 days |
| Hike on stilts 31 miles per day for | | 58 days |
| Squat on a pole for | 10 days 14 hrs. 34 mins. | |
| Parachute jump from | .. | 30,800 feet |
| Have a family of .. | .. | 44 children |
| Live with heart stopped for | | 20 minutes |

**120° C.**

**74,000 ft.**

**−75° C.**

**20 mins. 5 secs.**

**130 decibels**

**22 days**

**75 days**

## by Corp. T. J. Campbell

# There Aren't Many Like That

I WAS lying in bed thinking of new ways to attract sister's attention when they brought him in and put him in the next bed. He didn't speak, but I could see he was awake, so after a while I asked, "What are you in with?"

He said, "Compound fracture," and I could see it was his leg, so I asked, "Motor cycle?" because most of the compound fractures are motor cyclists, but he answered:

"No. I was on a ship." Then he shut up and didn't say any more.

When the night nurse came on I learnt that his first name was Joe and he was a merchant seaman who sailed in an oil tanker that struck a mine, and that Joe and another man were the only survivors. The night nurse, who reads a lot, said: "The rest got trapped when the tanks exploded and perished in a boiling sea," and I told her not to talk like a twopenny novel.

The next day Joe and I talked quite a lot, but he never mentioned the boat. I found out he was 22 and single, but when he was coming out of the ether I learnt that doesn't make much difference to a sailor. Being single I mean.

After a time they let Joe get up with his leg in plaster and we went out together. Then the doctor told us we were to be moved to an annexe of the hospital in the country where they send patients that only time can heal.

On the morning we were to go a car arrived for us. The driver was a man in a grey suit who laughed too much and reminded me of a bookie who used to stand at the corner of our street until the whole tenement backed a long shot that came up.

When we got clear of the traffic I asked:

"How long will the journey take?" and he said that it all depended on the route we took. He said that normally it was only twenty-four miles, but if we'd like a spin he could make it last about three hours.

I asked about the petrol and he said he'd never had his tank

checked, and last time he'd registered a hundred and twelve miles
for the return journey—next week
he was going to a place on the
hills to pick blackberries for his
wife.

He went on telling us of the
trips he'd made and how he was
a full-time A.R.P. warden, but the
town never had a raid and this
was an extra job to help out the
hospital. He got all swell-headed
telling us of the petrol he used
with no questions asked, and
finished up asking us again if we'd
like a spin and not to worry about
the juice.

When he finished it was very
quiet in the car and we could
hardly hear the engine; then Joe
give a kind of a sob and spoke
to the driver. He said:

"Go straight there." Just that,
"Go straight there," and I could
see his face was very white.

The driver slackened his tie a
bit with his left hand and "What's
the matter, doesn't he feel well?"
and I said, "He's a very sick man."

So we went straight to the
overflow part of the hospital
where they send patients that only
time can heal.

I didn't look at Joe till we got
out of the car and then I saw his
face was still white and he looked
very tired.

"There aren't many like that,
are there, Corp.?" he asked, and
I could see a hell of a lot depended
on the answer.

"No, Joe," I said, as comfort-
ingly as I could. "There
aren't many like that."

*"Oh, very well, then . . . Adolf."*

*"I keep forgetting – is it up and along or down and across in hara-kiri?"*

## by James Boswell

# The Land of the Scorpion

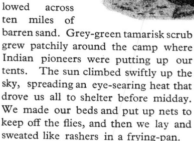

THE Middle East hit the new arrival right between the eyes. It staggered him with new smells, new people, new ideas. Two years ago our armies, streaming back to the canal zone, packed the camps, canteens and cities. Kiwis, Indians, Negroes, Afrikanders, Greeks, Poles, French and English jostled each other over crown-and-anchor boards, filled Shafto's ramshackle cinemas, and drank the Naafis dry. Threaded through this cosmopolitan mass, and giving it unity, ran the Rommel legend.

At every table and in every tent, the talk came round to Rommel; to his generosity to prisoners, his wisecracks about the British, his dash and skill and cunning. A few months later the legend was dead. And the tales told were about Monty's skill and dash and cunning.

But for us in Iraq, who left Egypt hurriedly to set up a hospital, the victories over Rommel were something we read of in out-of-date newspapers, or heard in bits and pieces when we could get the wireless to work. Heat, dust and boredom were our enemies, and transit camps were our homes while we waited for the hospital site to be made ready

Where the lorries dropped us in the sand, there were a couple of sheds built of mud and wicker, and a tap that stemmed off the water-pipe we had followed across ten miles of barren sand. Grey-green tamarisk scrub grew patchily around the camp where Indian pioneers were putting up our tents. The sun climbed swiftly up the sky, spreading an eye-searing heat that drove us all to shelter before midday. We made our beds and put up nets to keep off the flies, and then we lay and sweated like rashers in a frying-pan.

\* \* \*

WE stayed there ten weeks—maybe it was longer—we forgot days and dates, and each day at ten o'clock we went to our beds and lay sweating and cursing softly at the heat. Some slept. We told each other the stories of our lives, raking through dusty shelves of memory for fresh tales, to spin out the paralysing tedium of the siesta. In the evenings, when the moon hung improbably large above us, we sat around and tried to write home. We paid calls on neighbouring tents, and, if we were lucky enough to get the transport, a truck took us ten miles to the open-air cinema, to see a three- or four-year-old film. Through the flickering beams of light from the projection room, bats flew swiftly to and fro, dodging the changing rays and throwing sudden shadows on the screen.

At night scorpions crept under our ground-sheets and into our empty boots. One day the men caught a spider. A colossal chap, "a tarantula!" Maybe it was. Anyhow it was big and hairy, green, the colour of the tamarisk, and with a reputation for being poisonous.

The corporal called me over to have a look. A scorpion lay, still and braced in the corner of a petrol can. The spider moved a little to the left and to the right, not fast, but like a boxer who weaves to conceal his next blow. Then he leapt. One swift scurrying wrench, and out again. The scorpion had lost a claw, and his tail curved up over his body stabbing absurdly towards his missing limb. The spider leapt again, and tore off the other claw. The third time he went in to kill, and after the kill he ate the scorpion.

Ten minutes later he killed and ate another, and four shiny black claws lay around him, but he didn't try to eat them. The third scorpion was too good for him. He was getting slow. It stung him swiftly and retired to another corner. The spider didn't move much after that. Just lay and curled up slowly. The corporal shook the tin and he rolled over.

"He had it that time," he said.

Behind us someone said "Same as the dogs, see. Can't do anything on a full belly. Pound o' steak will lose you any race."

When the heat began to ease off, the dust came. At first, sharp little scurrying gusts, that whipped up fine sands and sifted it through the windows and crevices of the tents into the eyes and nostrils. Then, later, a steady pressure of wind that bore a

*Outside the cookhouse: "Greyhounds for dinner"*

*Visiting another tent " Telling each other the story of our lives"*

burden of fine grey dust filling the air all day. The sun became a butter-coloured disc, shadows disappeared, colour died, and at times a dim tangible dusk came down across the desert. Dust seeped steadily through us. It sought out every entry to our tents, stuck on our sweating skins, caked our faces, filled our hair, and, with a gentle interminable pressure, wore our tempers to a thin fragile membrane of sense.

*       *       *

EACH morning a thirty-hundred-weight pulled into camp, and three of us, from the ration store, climbed in. The Corporal rode in front. He knew the way and, though he couldn't speak a word of Urdu, he usually managed to guide the Mahratta driver to the depot. In fact he usually managed to get most of the things he wanted, and carried on a diplomatic offensive on behalf of the unit that kept us better-fed than we deserved.

We bumped along the desert track, marked out sketchily by old petrol cans with palm leaves sticking out of them. Behind us our dust cloud rose billowing in the upward currents of hot air.

After about forty minutes' run we hit the depot. Tents, brick sheds, mud huts, wicker herds, miles of basted wire fencing, pipelines for water, light-gauge railways, straggle over the level impersonal sand, in no recognisable pattern. Arab road-making gangs work casually, and beside a mud hole a brickmaker is slapping *motti* into a mould, and tipping out brick after brick in long rows. Inside compounds piled with stores Indian sentries keep watch from tall wicker-roofed platforms.

Our driver nosed his way down deep-rutted sand tracks, into the compound where we drew our vegetables. Aubergines, cucumber, bhindi, cans of dehydrated potatoes that rattle drily as you lift them. Archie disappeared round the back of the tent, and turned up again with a buckshee melon. Archie has a talent for getting buckshees. Sometimes I wandered round and watched him show his enormous biceps and barrel chest to the delicately-built Indians. They would come forward shyly and touch him—I was never very sure whether the melons were offered in admiration or conciliation.

In the butchery we stood and watched little, long-haired Indians at work in the slaughter-house. Their loincloths hung down, slack and heavy with sweat and blood. And from the shed, darkened to keep the flies away, their teeth gleamed white as they grinned back at us.

We drew half-a-dozen carcasses, so thin and small that we could take one under each arm. Sometimes we got Australian beef, and the truck drivers would go glum and silent on us when they saw it go on board. But nearly always it was mutton, and the cooks would greet us with bitter disgust when they saw the rigid carcasses under the net covers. "Christ, greyhounds again!"

\* \* \*

Month after month, in one place or another, the wide-curving circle of sand circumscribed our lives, setting a pattern for their monotony and helplessness. The future and the past became remote but infinitely desirable, as we learnt to live on our own resources, making the best we could of the present. And if there is any comfort in the thought, we knew, before long, that nothing we could do would change the austere face of the desert, and, soon after our departure, wind and sand would once again impose their shape on the deserted landmarks of the Army.

## by Richard Bennett

# Mess Meeting

"**A**NY comments on last week's food?" asked the Messing Officer.

The other members of the messing committee, five gunners and the Sergeant-Cook, looked at one another. They met every week to make constructive criticisms and plan for the future.

"Coal in the porridge, Tuesday," said the delegate from Headquarters.

"It's that kitchen orderly," said the Sergeant-Cook. "He gets carried away."

"Watch him, Sergeant," said the Messing Officer. "Anything else?"

"The potatoes are mouldy."

"Not enough bread."

"Meat's all fat."

"Rice half cooked, Friday."

The representatives of A, B, C and D troops spoke almost simultaneously.

"H'm," said the Messing Officer. "Everything else all right?"

The delegates nodded assent. "Good work, Sergeant," he said. The Sergeant looked pleased. "Next point on the agenda, suggestions for the coming week," said the M.O.

"Eggs," said the member for D troop, Gunner Ferguson. "More eggs."

"You've had an egg a week for the past two months. That's more than the civilian ration that you'd get at home," said the Messing Officer.

"I had two eggs a day when I was on leave," said Gunner Ferguson.

"You're a married man," said the Sergeant. "You eat your kiddies' eggs."

"I do not."

"It's the only way you could get so many."

"That's right. I'm a family man myself," said the representative from C troop. "But I wouldn't do a mean trick like that." He glared angrily at Gunner Ferguson.

"Order, order!" cried the M.O. "Stick to the agenda." But all eyes had been switched to Gunner Ferguson's face. He looked round steadily.

"Suppose we get them from the old man, my father," he said in an aggrieved voice. "Suppose he's on the Black Market. Eggs, fruit, meat, fish. Suppose we can get everything we want from him." Martyrdom and false accusation bravely borne gleamed dully in his eye. An apologetic murmur ran round the table. "It's not fair, sir, to say I eat the kids' eggs," he said to the Messing Officer. "We get them from my father. He's a big man on the Black Market."

The meeting broke up in silent embarrassment. "Unfortunate, most unfortunate, Sergeant," said the Messing Officer as they walked out after the others. "I really think that perhaps you should apologise to that fellow."

# DISCOVERY

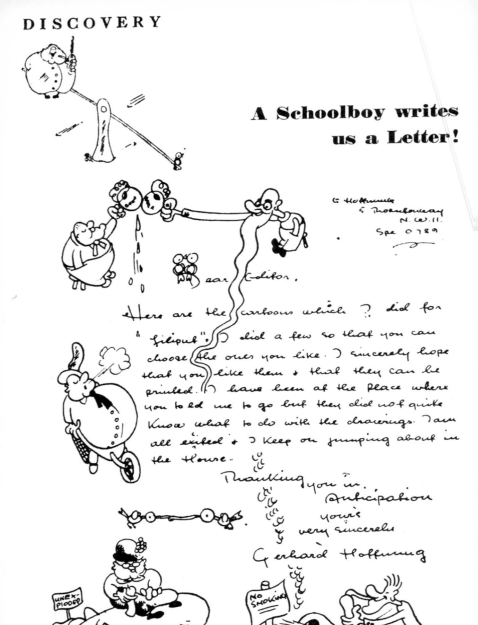

## A Schoolboy writes us a Letter!

G. Hoffnung
5 Thornton Way
N.W.11.
Spe 0789

Dear Editor,

Here are the cartoons which I did for "Lilliput". I did a few so that you can choose the ones you like. I sincerely hope that you like them & that they can be printed. I have been at the place where you told me to go but they did not quite know what to do with the drawings. I am all excited & I keep on jumping about in the House.

Thanking you in Anticipation
yours very sincerely
Gerhard Hoffnung

UNEX-PLODED

NO SMOKING

# ... and here are the Schoolboy's Cartoons

"And this is my husband"

"Oh! Speak Again, Bright Angel"

"I'm Nobody's Baby"

Hyde Park Orator

The Boy Who Knew the Answer

# CHARACTER

by John Betjeman

# In Praise of Dirt

ONCE I used to wallow in a hot bath every day. I admit that I didn't do much washing in it. I used it for thinking and for shaving when the weather was too cold to be standing up in naked air. Those sybaritic times are over. I am posted to a cold climate where there is a fuel shortage, and I am lucky to get one bath a month: and then the water comes out tepid. My skin has developed a protective coating after the manner of the Tibetans who, I understand, never wash at all, so that they do not have to wear vests. The result is that, instead of catching a cold once a fortnight from October to May, as I used to do in the old days, I only catch one once a month, after bath night. This is the only hygienic argument in favour of dirt: all my other reasons for liking it are æsthetic.

But before I come to them, it is fair to outline some of the horrors of cleanliness:—

The house where they put down newspaper over the carpet in the hall and in the parlour, so that you shall not bring mud in;

The room where you are offered a cigarette but where there are no ash-trays—only paper flowers in the grate and everything so much in order that there is no obscure corner where you can drop ash and a cigarette end without being noticed;

Taking books out of cases, rubbing the backs off with a duster, and replacing them upside down;

The habit of "turning out" a room which is in an order you understand, though it may look like disorder to the spring cleaner;

Cleaning and polishing linoleum so that you fall down on it;

Cleaning 18th century monuments in a church with a scrubbing brush so that all the fixture of the marble and the colour from the lettering is scrubbed away;

Cleaning ornaments which look better when obscured by dirt.

Not that I have any objection to people removing yesterday's cabbage from the interstices of a fork, or cleaning a visitor's lipstick off the rim of a tea-cup. My arguments against cleanliness are purely practical.

And when it comes to dirt, there is so much to say in favour of it, that it is hard to know where to begin.

How often have I seen a pretty face ruined by too much washing! Out of a factory or a farmyard there comes a girl in her working clothes, freckled face, tip-tilted nose, and a smudge on her cheek. She is full of character. An hour later she appears dressed up for the evening out. She has rubbed her cheeks in linseed oil, hidden her freckles under powder, removed the smudge and painted her lips, and she looks just like every other girl on an evening out. She has no character left at all: she looks no more than a sepia photograph in the fashion pages of a woman's magazine or, worse still, one of the colour plates.

The same argument applies to toys. My little son has a Teddy bear. When it was given to him two years ago it had no character at all: glass eyes and an expression like an inexorable Civil Servant. Two years of affection have worn away some of its fur and flattened out the rest, the glass eyes have been replaced by woollen ones, a grey film has appeared on its forehead and nose so that the dear old thing is now full of character and looks like a benevolent Beefeater.

I am told that in the wine trade, when there was wine to be sold, unscrupulous merchants would spray rubber solution on bottles which looked too new, so as to give them the vintage appearance of being hung with cobwebs. To this day the same principle applies (in terms of genuine dust instead of take cobwebs) to the antique and second-hand book trades. I, for one, would never buy old books or furniture if they were all smartened up and clean. I would think that I was going to be charged too much for them and that I would be paying a tax to the interfering brute who had bothered about them enough to want to remove the dirt. The shrewd dealer reckons on dirt to make people think he doesn't know the value of what he is selling.

Many places depend on the dirt in them to make them hospitable. What

is more naked and ashamed than the public house when it has just opened its doors? There are the shining floor, the ash-trays empty, the windows steamless, the bar glistening and deserted, the palms quivering from their wash, and the whole place reeking of disinfectant. He is a confirmed dipso who can give the first order in such an atmosphere, a nicotine-fiend who can light the first cigarette. But in two hours' time cigarettes have been trodden into the sawdust, beer lies in rings on bar and tables, crowds thicken, voices rise, the piano begins.

Yet of all the beauties of dirt, the most beautiful is dirt on buildings. "Dear, old, dirty Dublin," "Dear, old, dirty London," "Dear, old, smoky Manchester." You will notice how "dear" goes with "dirt" and "smoky." You couldn't say "Dear, old, dirty Welwyn Garden City" or "Dear, old, dirty Bournville," because they aren't dirty and they are not "dear." I notice when I return to London that it has not been painted for some time. Stucco has even more grace as it peels from late Georgian terraces; neo-Georgian banks and post offices are mellowed down by smoke from staring red to smoky golden-brown: even those ghastly cliffs of commercial-Renaissance in New Regent Street look a little less pretentious and a little less forbidding without their annual wash.

They can never take on the exquisite texture of black and silver-white which smoke of centuries has given to Wren's Portland stone churches and Cathedral, but they look much better than they will when their owners wash them after the war

I do not know what particular kind of dirt has given the Georgian squares and terraces of Dublin the Guinness-washed reds and browns of an old aquatint. But dirt has transformed those miles of brick into miles of elegance.

The fog descends on Manchester. It blackens the old Cathedral, it blackens many a Victorian church and Venetian-Gothic warehouse until they, too, begin to look as venerable as the Cathedral itself. It will, please God, blacken the new Library.

The mists from the Mersey wrap round Liverpool, the new estates begin to look less hygienic and more habitable, St. George's Hall is blacker and grander than ever, the Royal Liver building greyer and more extraordinary.

Time's dirty fingers touch the towns with texture. And they do not forget the country. At Bourton-on-the-Hill, no one has been along with a long-handled broom and brushed the flaking stone from wet Cotswold roofs. Moss has grown in the dirt and brought more dirt and grown more moss. Uneven stone roofs are gold and black and green.

I am coarse of mind, coarse of texture, a prey to most of the vices to which man is subject; but the one kind of dirt I do not enjoy is the dirt of the dirty story. It breaks up consecutive thought, it muddles conversation, it is generally apropos of nothing. A braver man than I am says to people who try to make themselves pleasant with this form of dirt: "Do you know me very well?" "No." "Then what right have you to tell me that story?"

And now I hear the water running for my monthly bath.

# Bernard Shaw Advises a Young Writer

## A Youth writes:

*Dear G.B.S.,*

I am on the Thames Embankment, and it is six o'clock at night. The tide is high, and the water is chopping in a cold wind. A barge is passing under Charing Cross Bridge, and a man on deck is blowing his hands. There are people in overcoats walking this way and that, and I am facing the river. I am leaning on the wall, writing this letter to you.

You are walking up the steps of the bridge, and you have a walking-stick. You also have a red nose, and you are very old. But you are strong and successful, and you are clever and you are rich. And I am a young man, leaning on the wall of the Thames Embankment, wanting to write. And I can't do it, because the wall is cold, and the wind is cold, and my pencil is small, and my hands are numb.

You are now in the middle of the bridge. You are standing against the parapet, and you are staring into the seventh dimension. And the people are hurrying past you from their city desks. And they are all in a mighty hurry to get home.

G.B.S., I am very cold, and I have no place to work. My landlady has a tongue and she talks about clothes coupons and jam preserving, and I am

not interested. You have a flat in Whitehall Court, and I would like to use it.

Very faithfully, *Alfred Ridgway.*

\* \* \*

## G.B.S. replies:

*Dear Mr. Ridgway,*

For domestic reasons which I need not go into, your plan is not practicable. Even if it were, I should not advise you to accept it. Such arrangements always lead to complications that are very undesirable, unless you can live with a resident family as virtually an adopted son.

What is your age? If you are 21 there is no difficulty. On your references you can get a reader's ticket at the British Museum and make the Reading Room your daily refuge, as I did for many years, and Samuel Butler and Karl Marx did all their lives. You must write your fiction with pen and ink, as typewriters are not allowed except in the newspaper department; at least, they were not in my time. Quiet is compulsory, and the seats and desks very commodious; if you cannot write there you cannot write anywhere. Much of my work has been done in railway carriages and on bus tops.

You should learn phonetic shorthand, not reporting shorthand, which would take you years to master, but learner's shorthand, which you can write at your ease and have transcribed and typed by a secretary as I do when you can afford one, or by yourself when you can't. To report, you have to be able to write 150 words a minute. To write as you compose, 12 words a minute is ample, as you can write slowly and legibly. Dickens, who began as a reporter, had to write all his books in longhand, as his reporting script could not be read by anyone else, nor by himself for very long. You can teach yourself Pitman's alphabet, and the ticks and dots for the prepositions, conjunctions and pronouns, in a few weeks.

Live near the Museum if you can.

There are other libraries: the Guildhall, the Victoria and Albert, and others which you might find out about if you are under 21. But in that case what about your military service?

Faithfully,

*G. Bernard Shaw.*

GON TO LYNCH BACK AT 4

Ronald Searle

## The Mysterious Lodger

The extract on page 82 is from *"Der Fuehrer"* by *Konrad Heiden*, published by Gollancz.

## by C. S. Forester

# The Eleventh Houri

MAYBE the Captain was a De Gaullist, and the ladies' husbands supported Vichy, and maybe it was the other way about. However it was, the eleven ladies found themselves the sole passengers in a little ship under the command of the Captain. In the colony which they had left an agreement had been reached by which the colonial government adhered to Vichy, or maybe went over to De Gaulle. Whichever it was, one of the terms of the agreement had been that these eleven ladies were to be transferred somewhere else. So there they were, on board this little ship, under the command of a Captain who was of the opposite faction.

Everything promised well, for the ship's course lay through waters so far untroubled by hostile action. Moreover, the food and the cuisine on board were far better than the ladies had had to endure for some time. They found a sheltered corner of the boat deck which would just hold their eleven deck chairs, and there they sat during the daytime, in order of precedence. At table, of course, the same precedence was observed: the wife of the Vice-Governor sat at one end, the wife of the Commissioner of Bridges and Roads at the other, and in the middle the wife of the Assistant Commissioner of Fisheries and Mines had opposite her Mme. Petit, who was the only woman in the company whose husband was not a government official.

THE pleasant interval of peace and freedom lasted only thirty-six hours. The second evening, at dinner, when they had finished their *blanquette de veau* and were far along with their chocolate éclairs, the Captain, cap in hand, came into the dining salon. At once the chatter died away, and everyone gave him full attention, for the Captain was a personable, youngish man, with a roving, humorous eye and one eyebrow permanently raised. The Captain acknowledged the concentration of the general interest on him, with a little bow.

"Ladies," he said politely, "I trust you are all comfortable?"

A little murmur told him that his assumption was correct.

"It desolates me, then," went on the Captain, "to do anything that will disturb your present tranquillity."

The women looked at each other with a trace of perturbation. But the Captain hastened to reassure them.

"It is the merest trifle," he said, "the most inconsiderable detail, and only one of you will be inconvenienced.

"I am a lonely man," went on the Captain. "Not since 1939, ladies, have I had the felicity of being in the bosom of my family. I yearn inexpressibly for domestic bliss. My nights are solitary, and my days are haunted by indescribable images. You will agree, ladies, that this is not a desirable nor yet a happy condition. I wish that one of you ladies would relieve it."

The wife of the Vice-Governor rose in her wrath. "Sir," she said, "your suggestion is despicable. Speaking for myself, and I am quite sure I am voicing the sentiments of all these other ladies, I must request you to leave this room which you defile with your presence."

There was a murmur of agreement when she looked down the table. Yet the Captain remained unabashed.

"Ladies," he said, "it never occurred to me that eleven such distinguished and beautiful women could all be as heartless as you seem to be. It desolates me to make that discovery. Moreover, it desolates me for another reason. As you are doubtless aware, ladies, the Captain of a ship holds certain extraordinary powers. His authority is quite unquestioned. Any passengers for whom I should find a distaste might be very uncomfortable indeed. They might be reduced to a diet of ship's biscuit and water. Instead of taking the air on the boat deck they might be confined in some compartment below the water line, where cockroaches abound, and where rats the size of fox-terriers run squealing through the darkness. It would hurt my feelings almost beyond reconstitution if I were compelled by the exigencies of my situation to condemn eleven women to such an experience."

That was a gloomy picture indeed.

The women looked at each other all over again, with new eyes. Finally the wife of the Vice-Governor voiced the question they all wanted asked.

"What do you want us to do?" she said.

"I would be grateful," replied the Captain, "if you would settle the matter among yourselves. I should be very embarrassed at having to discriminate among eleven ladies who are all so charming and amiable. If one of you, in half an hour's time, were to come and seek me in my cabin, I should not merely be satisfied, I should be emparadised. Good night, ladies, to ten of you. Au revoir to the eleventh."

AND with that he withdrew, leaving the ladies sitting over their only half-consumed chocolate éclairs.

"The insolence!" said the wife of the Vice-Governor. "The cruel, unspeakable arbitrariness!"

"Please remember, Madame," said the wife of the Commissioner of Bridges and Roads, "that his power over us is unlimited."

"Rats the size of fox-terriers!" wailed the wife of the Assistant Director of Posts, Telegraphs, and Telephones.

"Can we yield to a threat?" demanded the wife of the Vice-Governor.

"Yes," said the wife of the Superintendent of Public Education, greatly daring. And as soon as she said it it was evident that she had the sentiment of the meeting with her.

"One of us must sacrifice herself for the sake of the others," said the wife of the Adviser on Native Affairs.

"Then who will go to the cabin of this intolerable dictator?" asked the

wife of the Vice-Governor.

That question was not so easily answered. Nobody wanted to volunteer, for fear her motives would be misconstrued. There was a silence which endured for some time before it was broken by Mme. Petit, who, not being the wife of a government servant, was not so bound by convention.

"Let the cards decide," she said. "Deal one card to each, and the one who holds the lowest goes."

"So be it," said the wife of the Vice-Governor, grimly. The wife of the Commissioner of Bridges and Roads rose from her chair and brought the cards from the drawer of the card table against the bulkhead.

She shuffled them, and proceeded to deal a card face upward to each woman at the table. A ten, a knave, a seven. The wife of the Vice-Governor received the ace of hearts. Then the little wife of the Assistant Commissioner of Fisheries and Mines received the two of clubs, and a little sigh escaped from

ten pairs of lips.

"No need to deal further," said the wife of the Commissioner of Bridges and Roads, with decision.

The wife of the Assistant Commissioner of Fisheries and Mines sat still, her eyes cast down to the fatal two of clubs before her, and then, without a word, rose from her chair and ran from the room.

NEXT morning there were the eleven deck chairs on the boat deck. Ten of them were closely side by side, and all ten were occupied; the eleventh was empty and set a little apart, as was to be expected. The ten women were chatting pleasantly and indifferently, with only an occasional glance at the vacant chair.

The wife of the Assistant Commissioner of Fisheries and Mines, when at last she appeared, slipped unobtrusively into her chair, and made no attempt to close the gap that yawned between herself and the others. At luncheon, and at dinner, everyone contrived to sit at table with her without having to address her directly or even meet her eye.

Yet dinner did not go by without disturbance. That was more, really, than they should have expected, as they realised when the insolent Captain made his appearance once more, brazen and unabashed, with the same little bow and the same eyebrow raised higher than the other.

"Ladies," he said, "I hope you will forgive me for intruding upon you again. But another long, lonely night yawns before me. I feel myself compelled to ask you again to make a selection. I hasten to assure you, ladies, that I have not a word to say against my charming and delightful companion of yesterday,"—here the Captain's eyes met those of the wife of the Assistant Commissioner of Fisheries and Mines; "but the experience was so Elysian that I am tempted to see what other blessings destiny can have in store for me. I hope that among the ten of you there will be one whose heart will be softened, because the alternative that I mentioned to you yesterday still exists, and it would irk me beyond description to have to apply it."

"You mean," demanded the wife of the Vice-Governor, "that you want *another* of us?"

"Madame expresses herself with a crudeness that I should have thought alien to a lady of her breeding," said the Captain, "but with perfect exactitude nevertheless."

When the Captain had bowed himself out, the wife of the Commissioner of Bridges and Roads broke the silence.

"Well," she said, "shall I fetch the cards?"

The renewed silence gave consent. Once more she dealt the cards round, and this time the lowest card fell to the wife of the Superintendent of Public Education, who stoically rose from her chair and left the room without a word.

So next morning on the boat deck there were nine chairs, close side by side, and two set apart, in one of which was sitting the wife of the Assistant Commissioner of Fisheries and Mines, while the other was vacant. The delightful weather and the calm sea persisted. Life was good, and nine women chatted peacefully together. Then came the wife of the Superintendent of Public Education who arrived unobtrusively and sat down beside the wife of the Assistant Commissioner of Fisheries and Mines, well apart from the rest, whose conversation hardly wavered a moment.

Yet soon the wife of the Superintendent of Public Education stole a glance at the wife of the Assistant Commissioner of Fisheries and Mines, and received a glance in return, and it was not very long before they were positively chatting, and as they chatted they hitched their chairs closer and closer together, until at last the nine beheld the outcast pair chattering away together in low tones, their heads nodding and their hands gesticulating. And every woman of the nine wondered what these two were discussing in such animated whispers. Even at meal-times it was just as bad, with those two exchanging private glances across the table. They might be initiates in some very exclusive cult, from the airs they put on.

So when the Captain came in again the silence that acknowledged his presence had almost something of a hush of expectancy about it, and his statement that he did not want to be lonely to-night was not met by any verbal protest; and after he had gone and the lot fell upon the wife of the Deputy Governor of Prisons and Forced Labours, she rose from the table without hesitation.

NEXT morning on the boat deck there were eight deck-chairs in one group and three in another, and immediately a most animated conversation struck up among the three.

The morning after there were seven chairs in one group, and four in the other, and when the wife of the Sub-Chief of Railways arrived and was made eagerly welcome, the wife of the Vice-Governor took one look and turned away.

"Disgraceful!" was all she permitted herself to say.

That night it was the turn of the wife of the Assistant Director of

Posts, Telegraphs, and Telephones, which made the balance between the haves and the have-nots very nearly even; and the next night the lot fell upon Mme. Petit, and the balance was upset altogether—six eager women chatter-chatter-chattering in one group, and five glum women feeling rather out of things in the other. Next was the turn of the wife of the Junior Procureur General, and then that of the wife of the Adviser on Native Affairs, and then that of the wife of the Deputy Comptroller of Finance, so that one fine morning found the wife of the Vice-Governor and the wife of the Commissioner of Bridges and Roads left to themselves while nine eager women discussed the mysterious unknown subject.

Even then the curiosity or the æsthetic taste of the Captain was not satisfied. He came in at dinner and addressed his unvarying demand to the wife of the Vice-Governor. When he had gone the wife of the Commissioner of Bridges and Roads said:

"We had better simply cut the cards; low card loses, as usual."

"*No*," said the wife of the Vice-Governor, with unusual decision, "low card wins."

If the objective of the wife of the Vice-Governor had been to ensure the preservation of her virtue one more night, she attained it, for she cut a seven against a king. Yet she stood gazing down at the seven, fingering it and turning it over and over for a long time after the wife of the Commissioner of Bridges and Roads had slipped away.

It was not long before lunch that a change came over the situation, when a long, lean, wicked destroyer hove up over the horizon with the white ensign flying bravely astern. She exchanged a flurry of signals with the ship. The upshot was that the destroyer took the ship in to the port which lay just below the horizon. When the anchor fell the Captain came on to the boat deck with his usual lifted eyebrow.

"I much regret to derange you ladies," he said, "but the British authorities insist on taking you out of my guardianship. I particularly regret it, as I did not expect any such occurrence, at least not for another day. But one cannot argue with six-inch guns. I must ask you, ladies, to pack your belongings ready to go ashore instantly."

And when the time came to say good-bye, while the boat danced at the foot of the accommodation ladder, ten women shook hands with the Captain and wished him God-speed and good luck. The eleventh one was the wife of the Vice-Governor, who swept past him without a glance. Moreover, the ten had accustomed themselves to paying no attention to her, and even began to advance toward the accommodation ladder ahead of her. But with the imperious gesture of conscious virtue, she held them back.

"You are not fit to go in front of me," she said. "You are not fit to associate with me for one moment."

Abashed, they shrank back, admitting their fault. They were the pariahs now. The wife of the Vice-Governor sailed past them with her nose in the air, down the accommodation ladder, and took her place in the boat as if she were the only woman in the world.

*"Make way for a resident, you evacuee!"*

*The girls that got the fanmail*

In the first hundred numbers Lilliput published almost a thousand photographs including, or concentrating on, girls. We have never got around to adding up all the letters we have received, but the girl above (we called her "Babyface") was a clear case of first favourite. Perhaps because she'd be nice to keep a date with, perhaps because she'd appreciate your conversation. For the record, she comes from Dallas, Texas, U.S.A., and she was eighteen years old when the picture was taken. Her name is Frances. We forwarded all the letters to her, but we never heard if any of her admirers got results.

*Address unknown*
*We published this picture at the beginning of the war and called it "Land Girl." At the time we had no idea how popular land girls are: popular with everyone, but particularly with soldiers in hospital, land girls – and doctors – might be interested to know. This particular land girl came from Czechoslovakia. Not even Gidal the photographer knows where she is now, but he suspects she may be married. She told him she thought she was waiting to fall in love. He says if anyone comes across her they would recognise her at once, because "her name is Ursel and she behaves like a tiger cub."*

*The girls that got the fanmail – sitting shot*
*Once we thought we'd have to charter our own aeroplane to take copies of this photograph
to the Eighth Army. Perhaps, being in the desert, they liked the picture for the ice. "If
'The Girl We Met on the Ice' is English," wrote two Australian airmen, "believe me, there
will be a flock of Aussies visiting you after the war." The girl is Marie MacDonald, radio
glamour girl, a sporting type who likes riding and swimming first, skating last. She is also
America's Number One Sweater Girl – and likes to wear sweaters all the time.*

BLACK STAR

LO

*The G.I's dream of home*

## by Geoffrey Willans

# Homecoming

"WE can move along," said the G.I. "Yes, sir! We're rugged: we can take punishment."

That let the colonel into the compartment. I buried myself in a newspaper because, a minute before, I had squeezed him out of it. He was an austere little man, yet his blue eyes twinkled pleasantly when he smiled.

"Thank you very much," he said.

The train started with a jolt: outside it was dusk and pale mists were settling over the sea.

There was silence. We sat there dumbly, encased in ourselves. The British in a railway carriage. The G.I. squeezed the hand of the girl beside him. She was a pale girl with dark hair and eyes: beautiful but dumb, very dumb. She giggled at the G.I. and whispered something.

"Along the corridor," he said. "Just ask for Joe."

"She beats me," he told us, when the girl had gone. "Yeh, you ought to see the welts on my shoulders."

We smiled palely, but we smiled. The G.I. was unembarrassed. He turned to the colonel.

"You look sunburnt, sir."

The colonel smiled.

"In Karachi two days ago."

"Karachi? Yeh, that's not bad. Been away long?"

"Eight years."

Now the G.I. was impressed. Eight years! You could make and lose a million dollars in eight years.

"In the army, sir?"

"I have been in the army," said the colonel, "for twenty-seven years."

"*Twenty-seven years!*"

It was quite unbelievable!

"Why, if I was in that time I'd have hash marks up both arms. I'd be slaughtered: I'd be dead! I don't like the army, myself. Every Saturday there's checking parade and they tell us to cut our hair. You have to clean buttons for that. I guess some old colonel thinks it up."

The colonel smiled.

"I expect so."

"I'm certainly pleased you're home. Eight years! That must be great."

The girl came back and the G.I. kissed her.

"Honey, do you know how long the colonel's been in the army?"

The girl shook her head, blind with fright.

"*Twenty-seven years!*"

"England!" he went on. "Well, it's certainly a place to come back to. Other day I went over to—what's that place?—the Isle of Wight. Yeh, that's *really* beautiful—the white cliffs and the gulls, and the hills back of you."

He sighed.

"And I used to think Brooklyn a

land of sunshine and flowers!"

"Not," he said, "that there isn't plenty going on in Brooklyn—cops chasing people, women screaming or, maybe, just a robbery. I'll be pleased to get home there."

"Yes," said the colonel. "Home is home."

There was momentary silence.

"What do you think of the United States Army, colonel?"

No one dared breathe. The colonel cleared his throat.

"Efficient. Very efficient."

He had a concise, pleasant voice.

"Our armies have two points of view. Your people say, 'What do we need?': ours say, 'What have we got?' The American view leads, of course, to a certain wastage."

The G.I. handed his wife a chocolate.

"Yeh," he said, appreciatively. "There's certainly waste."

"I admire the British Army," he said. "Why, when I saw the way your Guards marched in Berlin! It was so perfect, I was *embarrassed!*"

"Last war," said the colonel. "Fifteen months' training before they put them in the line."

The G.I. nodded and patted his wife's hand. He was a nice, ingenuous type: half superman, half child.

"Mind you," he said, "I get mad at the British. Jeez, why not say so? I get mad at the queues. Take your wife to tea and there's a queue in the elevator. But what does it matter? After all, I got a wife out of the country that's not too bad-looking."

He turned and gave the dumb girl a fond kiss.

"There she is, wearing Yankee nail varnish and nylons. But there was lots of competition, wasn't there, honey?"

The girl sizzled something into his ear under her breath.

"George!" said the G.I. "Sure there was George! A British major! But I got her!"

He smiled round at us. He was full of good spirits and was doing the honours of the Old Country. He was welcoming the colonel home. The colonel said:

"Are you going back to your old job?"

"No, sir. But I've got seven hundred pounds in the bank and I take good pictures, so I should worry. I don't mind starting at the bottom, just like you did——"

"Me?" said the colonel. "Oh, yes."

I saw him chuckle to himself. Perhaps he was recalling those twenty-seven years of service.

And the trouble was that I liked the colonel. I, too, wanted to welcome him. I wanted to let him see—just something—that I knew how he felt to be home, that I knew what it must mean. But how?

It took some time but, at length, I leaned forward.

"Would you care to read the evening paper, sir?"

The colonel stared at me for a moment rather blankly. Then our eyes met and he smiled.

"Thank you very much."

"Jeez," said the G.I. "You should see my girl in a yellow dress with her hair done up!"

But I sank back content. I was pleased with life. I knew the colonel understood.

"No thanks, Old Man, I won't sit down – I'm getting out next drop . . ."

WHAT WILL BE DONE  IN THE EVENT OF AN

# INVASION

### BARRICADOES

Barricades for each street, to be defended by the inhabitants of the street; the corner houses to be supplied with hand-grenades, and for the more easy communication, passages should be made from house to house on the roofs.

## RINGING BELLS

A bell in the centre of each street, to summon the inhabitants to their posts.

## CELLARS

Night cellars in the City and St. Giles's, etc., to be examined, and every precaution to be taken that they should not harbour improper persons.

## OBNOXIOUS FOREIGNERS

All obnoxious foreigners to be sent out of the country.   No foreign servants, male or female, to be allowed.

# PRISONERS

Prisoners to be put into prison ships, in the most secure situations; so that they may be destroyed instantly, in cases necessary for the defence of the country.

## COAL HEAVERS

Every company of watermen, lightermen, lamplighters, coal-heavers, hackney coachmen, etc., etc., to be called out, in case of actual danger to the town, and magazines of arms to be placed in the Companies' Halls for their use. Fire-engines to be placed in proper stations.

From a pamphlet *"Hints to Assist in the General Defence, London, etc.,"* published on April 25th, 1798.

# VISIONARY

by Margot Bennett

## Post-War Problems

### Estate Agent

*Des. Det. Res., H. & C.,*
*Grge., Mod., Also Sun P.,*
*Gard., Tiled Kitch., All parq. Flrs.,*
*Spac. Nrsry., Snd. Prf. Drs.,*
*But do not rush to fill the empt. prams*
*There's just one hse. for every thous. fams.*

### Demobilisation

*The man who plans the rota*
*Will be by every voter*
*Cursed.*
*There are so many millions*
*Who want to be civilians*
*First.*

### Repatriation

*The American troops have returned to*
*the States*
*How quiet our rural areas have become,*
*Now the jeepless still town wholly*
*hopeless awaits,*
*The noise of English maidens chewing*
*gum.*

### Rhyme for Food

*The Argentine is short of cattle;*
*Brazil lies nutless after battle;*
*Will Mother Hubbard drop that grin*
*And tell the dog that times are thin?*
*The sugar cane grows short and sparse:*
*The Queen of Hearts can't make her*
*tarts*
*As before.*
*Will someone warn the sad Jack Horner*
*The queue still trails around the corner*
*Of the war ?*

### The Market

*After the war comes tin*
*Get tin!   Tin will be worth its weight in*
*gold*
*Bulls all will wallow in*
*Rubber—Rubber will fetch its weight in*
*gold*
*Prospects alas are thin*
*For gold—Gold won't be worth its weight*
*in gold.*

The cartoonist David Langdon answers our question: Happiness? What, no Hitler, no black-out, no gasmask, no sandbags, no war communiqués, no BBC home service! – How shall I make a living drawing funny cartoons?

# My Idea of Happiness After the War

We asked seven of the best-known British humorous artists to try to put into a drawing their idea of bliss when peace comes back again.

On this and the next three pages are the drawings they sent us.

*Vicky says: This is my idea of happiness – to have all the lights on at the same time.*

*My idea of happiness after the war*
*Heath Robinson's answer: To have a picnic like this*

*My idea of happiness after the war*
*Wyndham Robinson's answer: To draw this cartoon*

Maurice Hall answers:
That's what I would do . . .

Walter Goetz answers:
And that's what I would do

RESTORATION OF THE STATUS QUO IN: ABYSSINIA, CHINA, ALBANIA MEME CZECHOSLOVAKIA, POLAND, FINLAND, DA

And this is how Nicolas Bentley visualizes
happiness after the war: Back to the time
before the dictators

# CELEBRATION

## What They Were Doing When it Ended

### Nov. 11th, 1918

### An Ordinary Soldier

"ON the morning of the 11th of November there were rumours of an Armistice, but we did not attach much importance to them. At about 10.45 a.m. we were in action against the Germans, east of Mons, and one of our troops had just charged some German machine-guns. A private soldier came galloping towards us; he was much excited, had lost his cap, and could not stop his horse. As he passed us he shouted: 'The war's over! The war's over!' . . . We thought, undoubtedly, the poor fellow was suffering from shell-shock."

*Vain Glory*, Guy Chapman.

### President Wilson

"Many persons asked me what we did, and all I can answer is, we stood mute—unable to grasp the full significance. When confirmation of the actual signing reached the public, pandemonium

broke out afresh . . . At 12.45 we left for the Capitol, where the President (Wilson) made the formal announcement of the Armistice. At 4 o'clock we reviewed a parade of war workers, and at 8.30 drove out again to watch the celebrators. November 11th happened also to be the birthday of the King of Italy . . . We dressed and left the White House at 10.50 driving unannounced to the Embassy on Sixteenth Street. The ball, colourful with uniforms, was in full swing. . . The President toasted the health of the King and we stayed for about an hour. The day had been so crowded with emotion that we were too excited to sleep when we got back to the White House. So, kindling up the fire in my room, we sat on a big couch and talked until the early hours of the morning. Then my husband read a chapter in the Bible and went to bed."

*Memoirs of Mrs. Woodrow Wilson.*

### Winston Churchill

"It was a few minutes before the 11th hour of the 11th day of the 11th month. I stood at the window of my room looking up Northumberland Avenue towards Trafalgar Square, waiting for Big Ben to tell the war was over . . . The minutes passed. I was conscious of reaction rather than elation . . . And then suddenly the first stroke of the chime. I looked again at the broad street beneath me. It was deserted. From the portals of one of the hotels absorbed by Government departments darted the slight figure of a girl clerk, distractedly gesticulating while another stroke of Big Ben resounded. Then from all sides men and women came scurrying into the streets, streams of people poured out of all the buildings. The bells of London began to clash . . . My wife arrived, and we decided to go and offer our congratulations to the Prime Minister. But no sooner had we entered our car than twenty people mounted upon it, and in the midst of a wildly-cheering multitude, we were impelled slowly forward through Whitehall."

World Crisis. Winston Churchill.

★　　★　　★

" . . . *A distinguished writer . . . described how, at eleven o'clock on the morning when the Armistice was declared, he stood by his open window and listened to the solemn booming of the hour from Big Ben . . . But, as a matter of fact, Big Ben did not strike at all at eleven o'clock on that morning. When first the German air-raids began, the mechanism was disconnected . . . and it had not yet been linked up again. . . . Big Ben, however, did strike at noon that day, and no doubt our author heard it then.*"

Final Edition. E. F. Benson.

## Field-Marshal Haig

"On the 11th of November, 1918, Armistice Day, I was at Kingston Hill, and on my way to London to attend an important meeting in connection with the scheme for disabled officers'

clubs. I heard the bells ringing and the guns booming . . . Douglas, at the time hostilities ceased, was with his army commanders at Cambrai, and an enterprising photographer took them in a group for the cinema. Prince Fushimi of Japan with his staff, and Prince Arthur of Connaught lunched with Douglas in his train, and the former presented him with a Japanese Order. The Prince of Wales called on Douglas after lunch. The Prince was then with the Canadians, and was on his way to make a short tour of the battlefields."

The Man I Knew. Countess Haig.

## Hitler

"I was sent to the hospital at Pasewalk in Pomerania. . . In November the general tension increased. . . On November 10th, the aged pastor came to the hospital for a short address; then we heard everything. I was present and was profoundly affected '. . . so all had been in vain."

My Struggle. A. Hitler.

## Foch

"Two o'clock came on the morning of the 11th . . . Five minutes past— the Germans sent word they were ready. . . At five minutes past five, discussion finished. Five minutes later

the delegates affixed their signature to the agreement. . . At 7 o'clock Foch left for Paris 'with the Armistice in my pocket.' He called first to see Clemenceau and handed him the document with the words: 'My work is finished; your work begins.' Then, after a visit to Poincaré, he went home —to bear the good news to his family. 'It was a market day, and, while I was having my lunch, they saw my car standing outside. They then began a demonstration under my windows. So I went off. I was recognised in the Place de l'Opera. There was a bigger demonstration than ever . . . it seemed likely that they would drag me out of my car . . .' "

*Foch, the Man of Orleans.* Liddell Hart.

## Lloyd George

"London was deliriously celebrating the signature of the Armistice. The Prime Minister, who had given his blessing to this noisy rejoicing, himself showed a finer sense of the fitness of things. He spent the evening with his wife and daughter at a *Cymanfa Ganu*, or singing festival, at the Westminster Chapel, where he exercised his admirable voice in the rendering of hymns fitted to the occasion."

*Mr. Lloyd George.* E. J. Raymond.

## Margot Asquith

"The bell of my telephone started ringing, and taking up the receiver I recognised the voice of my American friend, Mr. Paul Cravath: 'The Germans signed the Armistice at 5.30 this morning and the War is over,' he said. I ran downstairs and gave orders for as many flags as could be bought, for the house, the roof, and the motor; and wrote three telegrams. . . It was a brilliant day and the sky was light. . . Henry and I felt it our duty to attend the cremation of a relative, and motored to Golders Green immediately after breakfast. I had never been there before, and was struck by the bleakness of the ceremony. . . . Nothing, however, could affect us seriously that morning. . . We arrived at No. 20 and found that our thoughtful butler had smothered the house in flags. . . I found my husband standing in the front hall holding a telegram (from the King). We looked at each other with tears in our eyes."

*The Autobiography of Margot Asquith.*

## The People

"On November 11th they said, 'We are so happy! We will show it and romp.' They did, and were happier still. On November 12th they said, 'We were so happy last night! We must romp again.' They made gestures more violent, lit fires, knocked hats off and charged each other in the streets.

"Were they happy? Perhaps. But I know I came between two men, facing each other, with the sulky semi-consciousness of bulls in their eyes, and with split lips and dripping noses. On November 13th they said, 'We must pump up jollity to the last dregs of all.' They rushed about, dragging cannon to batter in doors of hotels, tore clothes off the backs of women, and tied one, it is said, to a lamp-post and danced round her. I deduce that they were not so happy."

*Experience.* Desmond MacCarthy.

## Robert Graves

"In November came the Armistice . . . Armistice night hysteria did not touch the camp much, though some of the Canadians stationed there went down to Rhyl to celebrate in true overseas style. The news sent me out walking alone along the dyke above the marshes of Rhuddlan (an ancient battle-field, the Flodden of Wales), cursing and sobbing and thinking of the dead."

*Good-bye to All That.* R. Graves.

*"I only remarked that it had been a darned good meal."*

*The night we were waiting for*

ABNER WEBER                                                          LON

*Victory celebrations*

*Dream of home*

KEYSTONE                                                        LO

*Summer 1944*

*Summer 1945*

KEYSTONE

LON

*Homes for heroes*

YORK TIMES

*Cake for the party*

LONDON

POPPER

LON

*"Home is the sailor . . ."*

# Gulliver Celebrates the Peace

THE little Soho pub, where the crooks go, was making V-Day holiday. The dingy rococo ceiling was lined with Allied flags. The dingy rococo barmaids were lined with red, white and blue ribbons. The publican, lined in a silk shirt with his monogram worked into it and displaying an identity disc made out of a golden half-sovereign, oozed peace at every pore. Outside, a street musician trumpeted "There'll always be an England." And all the boys and girls of the underworld crowded happily into the little bar, throwing crumpled notes into the pools of beer, and drinking, with noisy enthusiasm, to peace and Allied victory.

The rejoicings must have come from the heart, as the plain clothes cop, who was keeping an eye on things in the corner, pointed out, because it was difficult to imagine how any of the regular patrons of this joint were going to make good: or, at any rate, do as well for themselves out of the peace as they had out of the war. But, on V-Day, the underworld, like everybody else, wasn't thinking of work, or the problems of the future. To the surprise of the police, the con. men, the smash-and-grabbers, the black marketeers, even the bottle party boys, celebrated V-Day in London with a spontaneous—well, an

271

almost spontaneous—stoppage of work. True, a confidence man was so inspired by the occasion that he actually succeeded in selling somebody a gold nugget (the first time the old dodge has been pulled off for years). But, apart from a few pick-pocketing incidents, crime was as rare in the West End of London on V-Day, as taxis.

## The Colonel's Camera

As the plain clothes cop said: it can only have been patriotic fervour that did it. Not since Armistice Day, 1918, has the underworld had such a marvellous opportunity to reap a harvest. Women didn't wait for the bag-snatchers: they literally threw their handbags about the place. But nearly all of them, when they called repentantly and unhopefully at the police stations the following morning, got them back complete with money and coupons. The underworld was as nice about it as that.

In the whole of V-Day, the plain clothes cop in the crooks' pub said that, only once, were "the boys" tempted. That was when an American colonel drifted in with an expensive miniature camera on his shoulder.

And, even then, "the boys" didn't think of themselves. They offered the camera—and, across our hearts, this is a true story—they offered it to the plain clothes cop as a V-Day present. They said to him "You're interested in cameras, Guv'nor, aren't you?" The cop said, yes; as a matter of fact, he was a keen amateur photographer. "All right," said the boys. "Just go outside a minute, and you can have that one." And the only reason the

cop didn't get the embarrassing present was because he wouldn't go outside; he knew "the boys" wouldn't pinch the camera while he was actually looking on. So, although the American was already "ganged" against the counter, although there was an open razor ready within a few inches of the strap, he didn't lose his camera after all. And he went out thinking how clever he was to get a drink on V-Day so quickly.

If you'd dropped in for a drink yourself, it's probable that you wouldn't have been any wiser than the American officer as to the company you were keeping. You might think that some of the customers looked rather tough. You wouldn't, unless you'd been celebrating in a big way, have pushed aside the scarred gentleman in a pin-striped dove-grey suit, who surprisingly was helping to carry the dirty glasses from the bar tables to the counter. If you'd enquired his function, you'd have been told he was "the minder;" meaning that his duties were to see that all the customers minded their own business. What you wouldn't

have been told is that the scars on the minder's face were razor slashes and that the minder himself was, in peacetime, a smash-and-grab raider. His war job is to drive fast cars round the country and carry off poultry and eggs for the black market. But, on V-Day, "the minder" was resting, and at peace with the world. All the tough customers were.

## Fun in the Streets

"Surely," we said, "it isn't all respectable."

"Depends what you mean by respectable," said the cop. "If you'd been in Piccadilly Circus last night you'd have seen a woman take all her clothes off and throw 'em to the crowd."

"What did the crowd do?" we said.

"They got somebody to put a searchlight on her."

"Anything else?"

"Yes. A Canadian climbed on top of a hoarding to get a better view, fell over the back of it down two stories of bomb wreckage, and finished up in an emergency water tank. He was in there half-an-hour before we could get him out."

"Was he hurt?"

"He'd broken his thigh, but he didn't know anything about it. He was quite surprised when we told him."

"If he didn't know he'd broken his thigh," we said, "how did he know enough to prevent himself from drowning in the tank?"

"He didn't know he was in the tank till we told him. He didn't remember anything. But the fact is he floated. Perhaps his pockets were full of ping-

pong balls."

"Have you had any trouble with drunks?" we said.

"Good as gold. We had one chap, in red, white and blue socks, who climbed a lamp-post in Piccadilly, and passed out when he got to the top. But it was all right. He stuck up there. And, after he'd had a bit of a sleep, we poked him down."

"Bonfires," the cop went on, "are what we have to keep a real eye on. This evening, for instance, in Green Park, they started burning the park chairs."

"Any particular reason?" we asked.

"Yes," said the cop. "Somebody said that, now the war was over, they wanted some nice new upholstered chairs in the park: so they started by burning the old ones. A tree caught light, too. And we had to call out the Fire Brigade. Then the crowd climbed over the engine and all the springs broke, and a man did an acrobatic act on the end of the escape ladder. The result is the fire's still burning.

"The street performers who do damn fool things, like standing on one leg and picking up boxes of matches with their teeth, they've made a packet. What they do is get a crowd by doing something silly, and they have stooges in the crowd to start throwing money at them. In no time, it becomes a game which all the crowd start playing. And "the boys" are picking up a packet.

## Introducing a New Glass Trick

"A clever idea," we said.

"Talking of clever ideas, I'll tell you something really clever. There's a spry chap round the corner here runs a little pub. He bought it for a couple of hundred quid during the blitz days when you could get anything for a song. And, in the past four years, he's made about thirty thousand quid. Do you know what he did for V-Day? He put up a big notice "Free Beer" and, when the crowds poured in, he said the beer's here but I've run out of glasses. Bring in your own glasses and you can have what you like. So

what happened? People went to all the places round about and pinched glasses, which they brought in to be filled up with free beer. When they'd drunk the beer they left the glasses behind. So, for the price of a cask of beer costing about six quid, this bloke collected enough glasses to keep him going for another year."

The crooks' pub was getting fuller and noisier as the night of VE2 drew to closing time. As he was talking I saw the cop eyeing the clock. The publican, out of his white silk shirt with the monogram on it, was looking at the clock and the cop, too. They were both thinking there mustn't be any accidents to spoil the most law-abiding two days in Soho's history. Suddenly, the publican faded out of the bar and, a moment later, he reappeared with the cornet-player from outside. The cop looked on wonderingly. The publican winked. The cornet-player, after imbibing a drink, played a march. The underworld cheered him gleefully. Then, solemnly, under the instruction of the publican, the musician, like the Pied Piper of Hamelin, stamped out of the bar up the street with the most notorious bunch of ruffians in London frolicking behind him like lambs. As the last one disappeared, the publican clapped an iron gate over the pub door as heavy as the gates of Pentonville prison. He'd closed, without a fight, dead on time. Even "the minder," through the pattern of razor slashes on his face, made a grimace that was nearly a smile. The victory celebrations were over. To-morrow, the underworld, like everybody else, would be back at work.

*Lemuel Gulliver.*

## by E. Arnot Robertson

# Peace Comes to a Ministry

IT was an average day, after Peace had been declared in Europe. In the Establishments Division, the senior officer in control of staff was busier than he had ever been during the war, not accepting the resignations of those Temporary Civil Servants who had better paid jobs waiting for them. True, hostilities had ended in Europe, but the blessedly nebulous "State of Emergency" remained. "Your tiny hands are frozen," he sang at them in a light baritone, between gusts of Permanent Civil Service laughter, and tried to remember whether this was a snatch from *Tosca* or *La Bohème*. Eventually he rang up the Middle European Section to make sure—all those Poles and Czechs and so on, they were very musical.

They knew it was from *Bohème*, but told him *Tosca*, because he had just turned down their request for three new A.S.'s (Assistant Specialists: a grade which, since VE Day, had risen in pay through bonuses, from a maximum of £400 per annum to £448) on the odd grounds that they were to be in charge of liaison with Russian-occupied Germany, so there was no one in the Ministry for them to be Assistant to, and nothing in which they could Specialise. "I hope I will let this be a lesson to me," said the Director of the Middle European Section

severely, translating out of the Norwegian which was his mother-tongue, for the benefit of M. Stacuynizski, head of the Swedish Section, "never to open again my mouth too narrow." The latter subsequently applied for, and got, three Specialists to manage Oslo (salaries, £500 to £700). Specialists were in order, because in the same Section the Typing Pool were all graded R.A. (Research Assistant). Specialists, in peace or war, come above Research Assistants by a minimum of £5 a week. There was a whole roomful of people to be senior to, anyway.

"Oh, my offence is Rank," quoted the Establishments Officer, as he signed the appointments, and immediately struck by the appositeness of this, rang up the Films Division to share the quip. It was unfortunate that no one there was in a mood to appreciate it. The great documentary about Men was nearing completion, and discussion raged as to whether or not to cut the controversial sequence: had experience in mixed batteries unfitted man for the home?

Apart from this, the picture was mainly a tribute from a panel of public-spirited women, who feared that in the praise lavished by the cinema on the part played by women in the recent conflict, the very real contribution of men to the war effort had perhaps been somewhat overlooked. So attention was called, in the visuals, to men's proven adaptability in taking on new jobs in war time; to the cheerfulness with which they had sacrificed such things as trouser turn-ups and pockets to the national good when necessary; to the stamina they had shown during long hours in the factory and in queues; special attention was paid to the problems of men over forty-five and it was hoped that the self-discipline of military training would not be wasted on those who must become, after all, the future fathers of the race. In the worst days of the struggle it had been a great comfort to women, said the commentator, a well-known doctor, to reflect that the men of Britain could be relied on to stand shoulder-to-shoulder with them, steadfast and comradely.

IN the Witch-doctors' Department, as the Religious Division was affectionately called, it was still being argued that they ought to have had a full-time Atheist on the staff to be truly representative: they had everything else. But it was felt—this had been the objection all through the war—that Atheists tended to be so dogmatic, and this had been one of the happy Divisions where everyone insisted that probably his colleagues knew better than he did himself on all matters of celestial preference.

"Dear old lad, of *course* I don't mind your having gone over my head with that Appeal to Air Affairs." One of the Scrutineers of Correspondence with Hostile Territories was repeating over the telephone, to a Scrutineer of Correspondence with Neutral Territories, what he had said at intervals throughout the war in Europe. "It's the sort of thing that just doesn't worry me personally. But for the sake of my Department I'm afraid I've got to lodge an Objection, Higher Up. You know how it is." Now, however, for the first time, he meant what he said. If you let your Department be overlooked, these days, one morning you came in to find you hadn't got a Department; and not everyone had better-paid jobs waiting for them, a fact of which the Senior Officer in Establishments was well aware. Then you came unstuck quite easily. "Haven't you seen the papers this morning?" said Neutral Territories, with ominous affability. "No! . . . You don't mean . . .? Announced, was it . . .? When do we . . .?" "Thursday week, dear old lad. Look, you'd better wangle a transfer before then. We've got a vacancy, only I'm afraid it means down-grading . . ." Hostile Territories, however, was no longer listening, he had begun the hopeless memorandum to Establishments, pointing out that as few of the Scrutineers had known German fluently during the European war, the fact that only two of them knew Japanese at all was no reason for precipitate action just now.

" What Stays had I but They, and they are Gone," murmured the senior officer sadly, as he accepted the appropriate file, labelled " Future Projects,"

from Scrutineers, ticked the memorandum, and removed the relevant papers to file E. stroke 79, stroke 3, labelled "Closed." The covers of obsolete files must always be used again. He pasted a square of white paper over the former label, and wrote on it, "References in English Literature to Bracken Growing Wild," on second thoughts marking this out to the Admiralty.

A small percentage of the staff, however, were leaving gladly, mainly those whose health or domestic situation, such as the presence at home of children under fourteen, had placed them outside the Essential Works Order. "On the whole, I'm awfully glad we stuck it out, aren't you?" A hairy man in Commercial Relations was comparing notes with a bald Anti-Liar, as they relinquished their Ministry Passes. (The Department of Anti-Lies had been one of the most successful efforts of counter-propa-

ganda, but now that Lord Haw-Haw was no longer in a position to broadcast, it was difficult to go on refuting him with the same precision.) "I mean, the temptation was pretty awful at times just to chuck responsibility and join one of the Services. Only if you've got any sort of special gift, you just haven't the moral right to, have you? But lots of times, when people simply didn't understand what a strain this sort of work is—well—I'll admit I've wanted to, haven't you?" "Oh, rather. I say, now we've left, would you think me a frightful copy-cat if I had some trousers made of just the same colour as yours? Only how does one get that sort of corduroy, with Nigel out of the French Section?" "Ask someone in Facilities. After all, we've been in this ruddy place long enough to get something out of it." "I shan't buy quite such thick corduroy though. It rustles so. Did you know the girls in Reference called you 'Lady Chatterley's Lover'?" "Yes —Urgh!"

Unfortunately Registry was having so slack a day that they had time to read, consider, and file all letters. If no appropriate file suggested itself to the thinkers, the correspondence was put aside for further consideration.

UNDISTURBED by the spirit of peace, Finance Branch carried on with its bitter and long-standing dispute with the Photographic Section over a bill, dated 1942, for half a ton of printing paper, on which—unaccountably—there also appeared the item, "Six Oranges." Finance, as had been pointed out in innumerable Minutes, was willing to overlook the fact that there had been no oranges in the country in 1942, so that if Photographic had incurred this unauthorised expense, the Section had derived no benefit from it: the point at issue was that the six were charged at a penny halfpenny each, and had there been any oranges in the country in 1942, the item must surely have come to more than 9d. "See previous communications: what were these oranges?" demanded Finance. "Round objects" wrote back Photographic; but Finance got them there. The minute returned to them the same day with, written across the bottom, "Who is Mr. Round, and to what does he object?" Absolute deadlock reigned.

In the washroom, near the main switchboard, the telephone girls were discussing whether Edna's nose got as red as Beryl's when she cried. It was agreed that Joy's nose hardly got red at all when she cried. Laura's nose, somebody pointed out, didn't exactly get red either, when she cried, but it was sort of swollen afterwards. Everyone felt that Christine was lucky, because you couldn't tell by her nose whether she'd been crying or not. No one discussed the reason for so many tears: after all, one ought not to leave the switchboard entirely unattended for more than ten minutes. Fortunately callers could only flash lights and not ring bells by their efforts, or no one would have been able to hear herself speak in the wash-room.

Meanwhile, tucked away in the corners of uncomfortably crowded rooms, oblivious to the clatter of nearly two thousand colleagues, seven or eight underpaid, overworked men who had carried the whole weight of the Ministry's job throughout the war, continued to toil as they had always done—swiftly, silently, and with quite enormous efficiency. As the battle of ideas intensified in Europe, now that

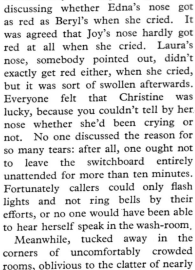

the war had stopped physically, they formed one of England's most important weapons, not so much secret as unsuspected; and even with the cost of their surroundings added to their salaries, they were probably cheap at the price.

### by Lawrence Benedict

# Demobilisation Blues

### Out, but what's it about?

No one, of course, would doubt me
If I said that the war could have been won without me.
But I wonder. Is, therefore, a man of my metal meant
To be fit for civil resettlement?
Can release
Bring peace?

### No room on the pavement

What can I do?  Where can I go?
I cannot reap;  I do not sow.
The recommended common task
Will never pay me what I ask.

### A cloud to every silver lining

It seems that business tycoons and caliphs
Hardly, if ever, have trouble with bailiffs.
But, oh what a crew! Even a bum
Is better company than some.

### Where we came in

Inconsolably we go,
Fearful, through this vale of woe.
They are wrong
Who say that women, wine and song
Can jolly us along.
Music, passion and the bar
Turn to sand and vinegar.
Nor is there a place on earth
For honest worth.

DRAWINGS BY JAMES BOSWELL

*"Now forget Arnhem, my boy, and come down by the stairs."*

**by Sydney Jacobson**

# The Stories They Tell in Berlin

BERLIN has a brittle gaiety you don't find anywhere else in Germany. The first winter frost may have snapped it, but up to now the Berliner has been making the most of his extra rations, his super black market, the autumn sunshine and the feeling that anyway there's nothing much he can do about it.

Having four Occupying Powers in one city has its advantages. Each of them is anxious to demonstrate its efficiency and civilisation, and the cultural competition is considerable. In the British sector, there is a fine smell of blanco, and plays by Shakespeare and Shaw; in the Russian, the plays are about Gorki and there are twice as many meetings and newspapers as anywhere else; in the French, the girls are beginning to tittup along the streets like Paris midinettes, and in the American everyone chews gum and there are some first-class dance bands. Grateful but not wholly convinced, the Berliner exercises his Cockney-sharp wit on all his conquerors, and goes on telling Russian stories.

Stories about the Russians are still as rife in Berlin as bomb stories in London during the blitzes. Time has taken the bitterness out of most of them, although they're still part of the stock-in-trade of the anti-Russian propagandists. A few are grim, many are funny, some are even true. The most typical true story I heard was from a small German business man, who was sitting gloomily at a table in the garden of his ruined house a few days after the fall of Berlin.

"A shadow fell across the table," he said. "I looked up and saw a great, hairy Russian with a big pistol in his hand. He growled at me in their atrocious German: 'Got any schnapps?' I said 'no.' 'Anything to smoke?' I said 'no.' 'Haven't you got *anything*?' 'No.' He grunted, said 'Good,' and lurched off. Ten minutes later he came back again. His pistol was in his belt, he had a bottle of schnapps in his fist. He said 'Get glasses.' I fetched two glasses. He pulled up a chair and filled the glasses. He said 'Drink.' We drank some schnapps. He pulled a handful of cigars out of his pocket and said 'Smoke.' We lit cigars. And there we sat and smoked and drank schnapps and looked at one another. When the bottle was empty, he got up, said 'Good' and went. A little later, a man who lives down the street rushed in. 'Man alive!' he said, 'I've had a terrible experience. A big, hairy Russian came in an hour or so ago, stuck a pistol in my stomach and went off with my last bottle of schnapps and a box of cigars.'"

Not all Berlin's Russian stories are as kindly as this, but a terror story nowadays is usually capped by two or three showing the Russians in a less horrific light. From an anti-Nazi Berlin lawyer came this picture of what the Russians' arrival meant to some Germans:

"There was house-to-house fighting in our street. We could hear the grenades bursting, and rifle-fire. We sat in the cellar and wondered when the first grenade would come. The fighting passed our house. We decided to come out. I opened the cellar door, and waited. The first to enter the house was a Russian with a tommy-gun. He pointed the gun at me. I thought it was the end. Then a Russian officer came in. He was clean-shaven and smiling. He put out his hand and said in German 'Good day. You needn't be afraid of us.' I took his hand, and at that moment I felt that my own 12-years' war was over."

APART from the Russians, some of the best stories you hear in Germany are unconscious. There was the waitress in a Berlin café who said reflectively: "It's been much quieter here since the S.S. stopped coming." And there was the war-time saying: "Make the most of the war, children, peace is going to be terrible."

Military Government humour,

too, is often grimly unintentional, at its best in the bar, half-an-hour before closing time. Then you can hear the problem of Germany summed up like this: "The difference between Berlin and the Ruhr is that if you give a Jerry a cigarette in Berlin he'll smoke it; if you give him one in the Ruhr he'll flog it for food." And you need not be surprised if the chap next to you suddenly says: "I'm the only man in the world who's got a receipt for a Krupp. I arrested the young one and handed him over to the S.I.B., and they gave me a receipt. I'd like to show it to you, but I keep it at home."

For cheerful urbanity, I give full marks to the loudspeaker at Charlottenburg railway station, which announced one evening: "Will the Release party at present celebrating by throwing empty bottles on No. 4 platform please desist."

But my favourite story came from the manager of a political cabaret. Among the audience were an elderly peasant couple. After a particularly virulent anti-Nazi number, they sat in silence for a long time. Then the man turned to his wife. "Old woman," he said, "I'm thinking it was Hitler they were talking about just now." Startled, she replied: "Don't be daft, man. They wouldn't dare."

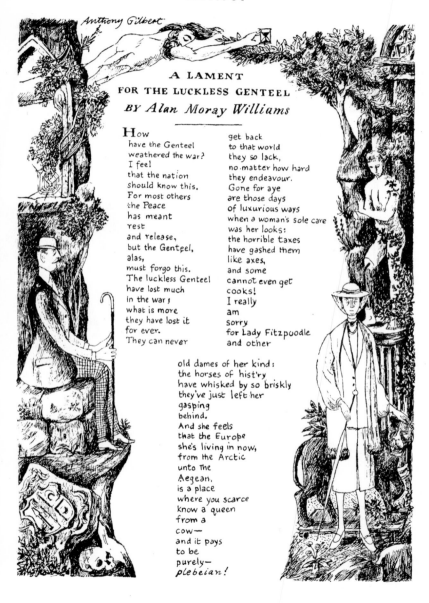

Anthony Gilbert

# A LAMENT
## FOR THE LUCKLESS GENTEEL
### BY Alan Moray Williams

How
have the Genteel
weathered the war?
I feel
that the nation
should know this.
For most others
the Peace
has meant
rest
and release,
but the Genteel,
alas,
must forgo this.
The luckless Genteel
have lost much
in the war;
what is more
they have lost it
for ever.
They can never

get back
to that world
they so lack,
no matter how hard
they endeavour.
Gone for aye
are those days
of luxurious ways
when a woman's sole care
was her looks:
the horrible taxes
have gashed them
like axes,
and some
cannot even get
cooks!
I really
am
sorry
for Lady Fitzpoodle
and other

old dames of her kind:
the horses of hist'ry
have whisked by so briskly
they've just left her
gasping
behind.
And she feels
that the Europe
she's living in now,
from the Arctic
unto the
Aegean,
is a place
where you scarce
know a queen
from a
cow—
and it pays
to be
purely—
plebeian!

"*I have an announcement to make. Jones Minimus here appears to have stumbled across the secret of atomic energy, so I must ask you all to carry on quietly while I go and see the Head . . .*"

120

10,000,000 prs.

# What We Could Have Had Instead

*In the one year* 1944–45, *the war cost us*

## £4,836,250,000

1,500,000

*Here is what we could have had instead*

5,000 galls.

|  | £ |
|---|---|
| 2 Ship Canals | 31,000,000 |
| 25 Giant Pandas | 20,000 |
| 4 Forth Bridges | 13,000,000 |
| 240,000,000 Bananas | 1,000,000 |
| 2 Cathedrals | 13,800,000 |
| 25 Greyhound Tracks | 6,250,000 |
| 100 Beauty Parlours | 500,000 |
| 12,000,000 Television Sets | 420,000,000 |
| 17,857 tons Milk Chocolate | 3,000,000 |
| 6 Under-river Tunnels | 12,000,000 |
| 1,500,000 galls. Ice Cream | 900,000 |
| 2,500,000 Candid Cameras | 75,000,000 |
| 10 Ocean Liners | 52,500,000 |
| 2,000,000 Labour-saving Houses | 1,500,000,000 |
| 20 Picassos | 120,000 |
| 1,500,000 Metrie Carat Diamonds | 4,196,000 |
| 1,750,000 Popular Cars | 437,500,000 |
| 40 Planetariums | 60,000,000 |
| 40,000,000 pairs Silk Stockings | 11,440,000 |
| 50 Art Galleries | 4,000,000 |
| 120 Goldfish Ponds | 72,000 |
| 4 Naval Bases (Singapore) | 200,000,000 |
| 5,000,000 Refrigerators | 195,000,000 |
| 1,000 grams Radium | 5,000,000 |
| 2,000 miles Trunk Motor Roads | 40,000,000 |
| 5,000 galls. Perfume | 240,000 |
| 1 year, 1 month, 23 days Freedom from Direct Taxation | 1,749,712,000 |

100

2,500,000

1,500,000 galls.

20

240,000,000

25

*"This Atom Bomb business will straighten itself out. You remember we had much the same sort of problem with body-line bowling"*

BOLONI                                                            PARIS

*The last function*

The editor and publishers wish to thank the following for permission to include articles, stories, photographs and cartoons in *Lilliput Goes to War:*

Richard Bennett (Lawrence Benedict, Margot Bennett); reproduced by permission of Curtis Brown Ltd (John Betjeman); Mrs Sue Birch (Lionel Birch); Marina Schinz (Blumenfeld); Ned Sherrin (Brahms & Simon); Lady Calder (Ritchie Calder); Michael Cummings (A. J. Cummings); Anthony Sheil Assoc. Ltd (Lionel Davidson); reprinted by permission of A. D. Peters & Co. Ltd (C. S. Forester, Arthur Koestler, Margery Sharp); Max Hastings (Gulliver); Alfred Rice (Hemingway); Lady Huxley (Julian Huxley); Lord Sydney Jacobson; Alan Jenkins; Paul Jennings; Olga Katzin; Cyril Kersh (Gerald Kersh); Lady Mitchison; Henry Moore Foundation; Mme Carmen de Polnay (Peter de Polnay); David Higham Assoc. Ltd (John Pudney, E. Arnot Robertson, Osbert Sitwell); James McGibbon (Stevie Smith); Tessa Sayle (Ronald Searle, Geoffrey Willans); the Society of Authors on Behalf of the Bernard Shaw Estate; Alan Moray Williams; Associated Press; Walter Bird Studios; Black Star Publishing Co. Ltd; Mrs Noya Brandt (Bill Brandt); Madame Brassai (Brassai); Tim Gidal; Christopher Glass (Douglas Glass); Akademie der Kunste der DDR (Heartfield); Keystone Press Agency; Mrs L. Man (Man, London); Pictorial Press Ltd; Popperfoto; Wolf Suschitzky; Topham Picture Library; Peter Hoar (Acanthus); John Yeoman (Anton); Mrs Barbara Bentley (Nicholas Bentley); Mrs Ruth Boswell (James Boswell); Mrs Eileen Brockbank (Brockbank); Emmett Revd Geoffrey Fraser; Walter Goetz; Mrs Annette Hoffnung (Gerard Hoffnung); Mrs M. D. Hollowood (Hollowood); Felix Kelly; David Langdon; Mrs Lee (Lee); cartoons by permission of *The Standard* (David Low, Vicky); Laurence Pollinger (Heath Robinson); William Scully; Kurt Maschler and the Art Gallery of Ontario (Trier); Mrs U. Davidson (Victoria).


Every effort has been made to trace holders of copyright material reproduced in this book. The editor and publishers apologise for any inadvertent omissions.

Kay Ambrose; Aszmann, Budapest; Pat Auld; Leslie Baker; Boloni, Paris; Bond, London; Chaddock, Liverpool; Dorien Leigh; Ernest; GF, New York; Anthony Gilbert; Gohler; David Graham; Maurice Hall; Stanley Herbert; Le Quay, Australia; Lisa, Welwyn; London News Agency; Norah Naylor; *New York Times*; Pitts; Rigner, Paris; Wyndham Robinson; Schall, Paris; Siggs; Starke; Stein, Paris; Tirtgens, New York; Geoffrey Wadlow; Abner Weber, London; W.N.S. London; Zeigler.

## How many pieces of leather in your equipment?

Too many? Not if you clean them in the quickest and best way. Propert's Leather & Saddle Soap is ready for use — a great time-saver — and it preserves the leather as nothing else can.

# PROPERT'S
## LEATHER & SADDLE SOAP

*Keeps leather clean and supple under all conditions.*

THE ARMY IS PROPERT'S BIGGEST CUSTOMER

# SMITH SECTRIC CLOCKS
*plug in to Greenwich time*

*A close shave!*

Also STEAD SILVER STEEL Razor Blades

# STEAD
## RAZOR BLADES
IN THE WEEKLY WALLET
THE BLADES LAST LONGER